Small
Gardens

Alan Titchmarsh
how to garden

Small Gardens

Published in 2011 by BBC Books, an imprint of
Ebury Publishing, a Random House Group Company

Copyright © Alan Titchmarsh 2011

The right of Alan Titchmarsh to be identified as the
author of this work has been asserted in accordance
with Sections 77 and 78 of the Copyright, Designs and
Patents Act 1988.

All rights reserved. No part of this publication may be
reproduced, stored in a retrieval system, or transmitted
in any form or by any means, electronic, mechanical,
photocopying, recording or otherwise, without the
prior permission of the copyright owner.

The Random House Group Limited Reg. No. 954009

Addresses for companies within the Random House
Group can be found at www.randomhouse.co.uk

Penguin Random House is committed to a sustainable future
for our business, our readers and our planet. This book is
made from Forest Stewardship Council® certified paper.

A CIP catalogue record for this book is available from
the British Library.

ISBN 978 1 84607405 9

Produced by OutHouse!
Shalbourne, Marlborough, Wiltshire SN8 3QJ

BBC BOOKS
COMMISSIONING EDITOR: Lorna Russell
PROJECT EDITOR: Caroline McArthur
PRODUCTION: Phil Spencer

OUTHOUSE!
COMMISSIONING EDITOR: Sue Gordon
SERIES EDITOR: Polly Boyd
SERIES ART EDITOR: Robin Whitecross
CONTRIBUTING EDITOR: Jo Weeks
EDITOR: Alison Candlin
DESIGNER: Louise Turpin
ILLUSTRATIONS by Julia Cady, Caroline De Lane Lea,
Lizzie Harper, Susan Hillier, Janet Tanner
PHOTOGRAPHS by Jonathan Buckley except where
credited otherwise on page 128
ORIGINAL CONCEPT DEVELOPMENT & SERIES DESIGN:
Elizabeth Mallard-Shaw, Sharon Cluett

Colour origination by Altaimage, London
Printed and bound in China by Leo Paper Products Ltd.

Contents

Introduction

Gardening is one of the best and most fulfilling activities on earth, but it can sometimes seem complicated and confusing. The answers to problems can usually be found in books, but big fat gardening books can be rather daunting. Where do you start? How can you find just the information you want without wading through lots of stuff that is not appropriate to your particular problem? Well, a good index is helpful, but sometimes a smaller book devoted to one particular subject fits the bill better – especially if it is reasonably priced and if you have a small garden where you might not be able to fit in everything suggested in a larger volume.

The *How to Garden* books aim to fill that gap – even if sometimes it may be only a small one. They are clearly set out and written, I hope, in a straightforward, easy-to-understand style. I don't see any point in making gardening complicated, when much of it is based on common sense and observation. (All the key techniques are explained and illustrated, and I've included plenty of tips and tricks of the trade.)

There are suggestions on the best plants and the best varieties to grow in particular situations and for a particular effect. I've tried to keep the information crisp and to the point so that you can find what you need quickly and easily and then put your new-found knowledge into practice. Don't worry if you're not familiar with the Latin names of plants. They are there to make sure you can find the plant as it will be labelled in the nursery or garden centre, but where appropriate I have included common names, too. Forgetting a plant's name need not stand in your way when it comes to being able to grow it.

Above all, the *How to Garden* books are designed to fill you with passion and enthusiasm for your garden and all that its creation and care entails, from designing and planting it to maintaining it and enjoying it. For more than fifty years gardening has been my passion, and that initial enthusiasm for watching plants grow, for trying something new and for just being outside pottering has never faded. If anything I am keener on gardening now than I ever was and get more satisfaction from my plants every day. It's not that I am simply a romantic, but rather that I have learned to look for the good in gardens and in plants, and there is lots to be found. Oh, there are times when I fail – when my plants don't grow as well as they should and I need to try harder. But where would I rather be on a sunny day? Nowhere!

The *How to Garden* handbooks will, I hope, allow some of that enthusiasm – childish though it may be – to rub off on you, and the information they contain will, I hope, make you a better gardener, as well as opening your eyes to the magic of plants and flowers.

Making the most of your space

In an increasingly crowded world, where 'big brother' seems to be looking over our shoulder at every street corner and the local supermarket knows our favourite foods better than we do, it is ever more important to have a private green space – no matter how small – that we can call our own. What a relief it is to step into our personal paradise, away from the bustle of everyday life.

What is a small garden?

It can be hard to define 'small', since it rather depends on your point of view. However, for this book it made sense to come up with a size above which a garden is no longer considered small and below which it most certainly is. For our purposes, a small garden is one that is no larger than a tennis court – an area of approximately 260 square metres (310 square yards).

If your garden is bigger than our maximum, don't be put off. Gardens are often best divided into smaller areas, or 'rooms' that could each be considered a small garden in its own right. Much of the information provided here can be adapted and used in gardens of any size.

Many gardens are more or less rectangular, though seldom as precisely proportioned as a tennis court, but gardens of all shapes can be made into beautiful places. In fact, even though they might appear a challenge to begin with, odd-shaped gardens usually end up being more intriguing, precisely because of those unexpected nooks and crannies.

Your outdoor space does not have to be level either: the most successful gardens created on flat sites almost always have at least one change of level incorporated specifically to grab or distract our attention (*see* pages 18–19 and 41–3).

Size is important
Always think of the small size of your garden as a positive thing. Small gardens can be created much more quickly than large ones. They can easily be redesigned, tweaked and experimented in; a few new plants, a simple rearrangement of containers or a change of patio furniture go a long way to altering the feel of a small area. Each plant in a small garden becomes a close personal friend and benefits from individual attention. Weeding, watering, feeding, pruning and tying in can be done in a matter of a few hours each week, leaving you with plenty of time to relax and enjoy your outdoor space.

On the downside, mistakes are much more obvious, yearned-for plants sometimes simply cannot be fitted in, and lack of room may mean that some of your more ambitious plans must be relinquished. You're also more likely to be overlooked by your neighbours, making privacy high on your list of priorities. However, with a little ingenuity, you should be able to create a haven that goes a long way towards fulfilling your gardening desires.

Beauty and practicality are combined in this small garden, which includes a simple pergola, well thought-out planting and a healthy lawn.

Basic design principles

Most of us know when a garden works as a whole and looks good, but we might not be able to say quite why it is so pleasing. A successful garden is rarely a happy accident; rather, it is the result of a number of different elements intentionally arranged to interact with one another. Although they're described separately here, all these elements need to be considered together to produce a well-rounded design.

Unity and simplicity

When you start designing your garden, it will be very easy to get carried away with all the things you want to include. The danger with this is that you end up with a mixture of approaches and styles, and the result is rather more chaotic than beautiful. Always keep the ideas of unity and simplicity in the back of your mind.

One of the easiest ways to achieve unity is to limit your choice of materials to one or two types. Choose paving and other hard landscaping that match or complement each other. This way, whatever else is going on in the garden, these will act as an anchor and provide a unifying theme. Remember to think about the style of your house too. If it is red brick, for example, you don't have to use red bricks for your hard landscaping, but do choose something – perhaps of a similar or harmonious colour or shape – that will blend with the bricks and look like it really belongs.

While there is nothing wrong with using straight lines and curves together, make sure they link in a satisfying way. Sometimes simply repeating the same motif can produce a sense of unity. For example, a circular patio might lead on to a circular lawn, the two linked by a pathway that echoes the curve of the circles or is perfectly straight.

Proportion and scale

In a small space, a few large features are better than many small ones. Once again, when you have lots of

> The simple lines of this pool are echoed in the opening in the wall behind. Careful planting unifies the hard landscaping elements.

things you'd like to fit in, it can be hard to restrict yourself, but you'll find this is what works best. Two or three big pots will have much more impact and look far more stylish than a dozen ill-assorted smaller ones. One tree, if you can fit it in, is better than three shrubs of a middling size. However, one large, eye-catching feature surrounded by several very much smaller ones will not work: the larger feature will dominate, making it hardly worth including the smaller ones. If you have a large tree, complement it with a seat, some tall perennials or another item that's on a similar scale but is, perhaps, horizontal – such as a path or a low hedge or wall – to provide a suitable balance.

If you're planning on having two main types of surface, for example paving and gravel, or grass and decking, make the areas that they cover different in size. A good rule of thumb is to devote up to a third of the garden to hard landscaping, with 'soft' materials doing the rest. Equal amounts of each will at best look uncomfortable, at worst, dull.

In a detailed and colourful planting a large-scale terracotta urn, with its strong and simple outline, imparts a sense of proportion and balance.

Space and enclosure

Some garden styles, for example the urban jungle (*see* pages 25 and 74–5), call for a feeling of enclosure, almost to the point of claustrophobia, but nearly always there should be a balancing sense of space, too. A shady area for seating could be emphasized by placing it next to an open area that gets the sun; and the feeling of enclosure is actually enhanced by the space beside it.

It's even more important to provide enclosure in a very open or closely overlooked garden, since this is the only way you'll have any privacy. Most of us never lose that childhood love of hiding places and secluded paths, so something that recreates this feeling of secrecy is bound to be pleasing, even if only in the form of an arch or small pergola.

Gaps in an enclosed space encourage you to look through them into the space beyond, while looking from an open area into a densely planted one can give a sense of infinity.

With a little care, a blend of open and enclosed spaces will enable you to blur the boundaries of your plot and make your small garden seem more spacious as well as more personal (*see* pages 16–19).

An eye-catching chair all but hidden in the planting provides an inviting secret spot for private reflection.

Surprise

It's fun to incorporate elements of surprise in a garden. Even if they only surprise you the first few times you see them, they will amuse you for much longer, and can be changed when you get fed up with them. Try nestling part of a wooden dinghy – fully planted – in a flower bed; use an old pew for a seat; or add a note of whimsy with a wooden ladder leading nowhere or an empty picture frame encompassing a view. *Trompe l'oeil* (*see* page 21) is an effective technique, as are strategically placed mirrors, which also make the area appear larger, or pieces of coloured glass. Turf or driftwood sculptures and woven willow houses also give pause for thought.

Among the colourful flowers in this exuberant garden, the bust on a classical plinth provides a calm focal point. The neat bed edging provides a frame for the planting.

Focal points

Focal points are spots that draw your eye when you gaze into the garden. All gardens, no matter how small, ought to contain at least one good focal point, and preferably several of varying intensity – but cram in too many and they will all lose their impact.

Focal points act like punctuation marks, slowing you down, making you look closely, introducing something of interest, distracting you from something unattractive, providing humour and generally enlivening the garden as a whole. They can be a large 'architectural' plant with a distinctive shape (*see* page 90) or almost anything else: a piece of sculpture, a mirror, a striking pot or chunk of stone; your

focal point could even be the garden gate, the patio or a shed (especially if painted a fun colour).

Consider focal points from every angle in the garden, looking back towards the house as well as out into the surrounding area – in the wrong place they might do more harm than good. For example, don't use a focal point to disguise something ugly, like the dustbins; instead, use it to

draw attention away from the eyesore to a more attractive part of the garden. Put the dustbins behind something so totally unremarkable that you never notice them at all.

Light and shade

Never underestimate the effects of light and shade in the garden. Make the most of them and they add an extra dimension that goes a long way towards increasing the sense of space. Distinct areas of light and shade are particularly useful for disguising the single plane of a very flat site and can create an air of mystery, even in a tiny garden.

From an area of darkness our eyes are always attracted towards light, so positioning something pale or shimmering at the end of a sunless passageway or shaded pergola – a birdbath or a silver-leaved plant, perhaps – will increase the feeling of distance and space. Make sure that this object, or plant, catches the light and seems to reflect it into the gloom. By contrast, a curtain of leaves hanging over a window that looks out into the garden adds unexpected shadows and makes the view more interesting.

Don't forget

The reflective qualities of water make it a brilliant addition to any garden. Whether it is in a pond or a birdbath, the water will reflect light into shady spots and its constant, shimmering movement will catch the eye and make a strong focal point.

The ever-changing reflections produced by water make it one of the most attractive elements in any garden.

The evening sun highlights the texture of *Stipa tenuissima*, an effective contrast with the hosta and neat hedge behind.

to cut back or remove plants when they become crowded, and this can happen in a surprisingly short space of time. Plant to allow room for growth and fill the spaces in between with short-lived annuals and biennials, plants in containers or decorative items such as quirky pots, seating and sculpture.

Texture

Because we're surrounded by it, texture is often undervalued, yet its contribution to the success of a garden is immeasurable. Envisage a flat area of polished granite, and then imagine the same space covered by pavers with raised lines, dips and dents, as well as the joints and grouting. Even if the pavers are of the most basic concrete kind, they will create a very different effect from the smooth and shiny granite, and this effect will disperse out into the spaces all around.

When it comes to plants, the variety introduced by texture is even more important. To create a sense of liveliness in a garden, plants with small leaves can be contrasted with plants that have larger leaves, while those with shiny foliage could go beside those with hairy foliage. For a calmer mood, make harmonious groups – maybe a collection of plants that all have large, soft leaves in rich and dark greens.

Time

What part does time play in garden design? Well, at different times of day the height and position of the sun will change the look of the garden. Clever positioning of a plant or other element to catch the rays of the rising or setting sun can produce wonderful effects, even more valuable because they're short-lived. For example, the evening sun shining through red leaves will make them glow.

The other effect of time is ageing. Plants grow and mature, and hard landscaping settles into its surroundings, growing moss and lichen and gaining character with age. It is difficult to predict exactly how a new garden will look in a few years' time, but it's sensible to allow for some alteration, particularly when choosing plants. It's tempting to fill an area so that it looks good straightaway, but you will only have

In this Mediterranean-style courtyard garden the emphasis on shades of green and leaf textures is perfectly balanced by the warm-coloured walls and deep dark pool.

A simple colour wheel shows the ways in which colours relate to each other. Colours that harmonize are adjacent to each other on the wheel, while colours that make good contrasts are opposite each other.

Plant *Humulus lupulus* 'Aureus' with *Clematis* 'Warszawska Nike' for a striking contrast of lime green and rich purple.

The pale blue flowers of *Nigella damascena* 'Miss Jekyll' work in harmony with the glaucous *Festuca glauca* 'Elijah Blue'.

Colour

Colour can provide some of the most exciting effects in a garden, but it often proves difficult to get it just right. It's a good idea to search for inspiration in other people's gardens. This will help with two of the most difficult aspects of colour combining: season of interest and plant height. You might well find that plant combinations that look perfect on paper in reality bloom at different times, or at such different heights that the flowers will never be next to each other. Be prepared for some mistakes as well as some surprises: unplanned combinations can often be just as satisfying as deliberate ones. Annuals are fun to start with, since they bloom fairly quickly and can be grown cheaply from seed (*see* pages 103 and 121). Check the packet for flowering time and plant height.

You may already have strong ideas about what colours you like, but to create a truly successful garden, you may well have to consider including some of your less favoured shades. It is possible to fill your plot with just one or two colours, but the result could be rather monotonous, and even a little unsettling. It's usually far wiser to choose a palette of contrasting or harmonizing colours; the colour wheel above shows how.

Don't forget

When choosing plants, most of us consider flower colour first and foremost ... but flowers are fleeting, and it is the colour of the foliage that creates the more lasting impression.

Colours next to each other on the wheel are harmonious, while those directly opposite are contrasting; either combination should create a pleasing effect. You can restrict yourself to one colour, but use varying shades of it, including pastels and stronger hues. Using collections of similar or the same colours in select groups around a garden – like a series of echoes – is an excellent way to ensure a sense of cohesion.

Harmony

A successful garden must be harmonious. This doesn't mean it has to be pretty or unchallenging – there is nothing soothing about the Grand Canyon or the Eiger, yet they sit in their landscape in a way that is entirely comfortable and, therefore, harmonious. On a more domestic scale, natural materials, such as wood and stone, always blend harmoniously with the plants, while painted wood or brightly coloured man-made materials are far more difficult to integrate. In the right setting they can be used to produce something harmonious – but you do set yourself a bigger challenge if you choose this route, particularly in a small space.

If you find it difficult to get to grips with the concept of creating harmony throughout the whole garden, divide the area up into smaller, more manageable parts and ensure that each section links satisfyingly with its neighbour. You might still end up with some clashes but, in limited numbers, these could act as focal points or surprises.

Habit and form

'Habit' refers to the way a plant grows, for example climbing, rounded, upright, prostrate; 'form' means its overall type – tree-like, shrubby or perennial, for instance. However, the two terms are somewhat interchangeable. When you're choosing plants it's important to think about their habit and overall form, along with the texture of their leaves and the colour of their flowers. Select a variety of shapes, such as mounded and upright, spreading and spiky, to create a garden full of interest.

Variations in plant height and shape introduce rhythm and balance. A basic but very successful trick is to think of the groups of plants as creating a series of

pyramids or triangular shapes. If there is space in your garden, try to include at least one tree or tree-like subject to form the apex of the triangle. Underplant this with two or three lower plants making the sides of the triangle – shrubs or larger perennials are ideal. Finally, furnish the base of the triangle with low-growing perennials, annuals and bulbs. Interlink other triangles of different sizes to build up the whole

garden picture, making sure that you incorporate changes of scale to vary the impact and provide interest. A narrow yew (*Taxus baccata*) or slim conifer that is underplanted with a prostrate rosemary or juniper creates the impression of a tall, thin triangle, or, for smaller spaces, you could create a pyramid from a foxglove (*Digitalis purpurea*) combined with primroses (*Primula vulgaris*) and bluebells (*Hyacinthoides*).

Colour, texture and form have been combined to perfection in this garden. There is plenty to look at but the overall effect is tranquil.

Making your space seem bigger

Although a small garden has lots of advantages, it can also seem … well, small. Quite apart from this being because space *is* limited, a sense of smallness can be heightened by your being able to see the boundaries clearly, being overlooked by the neighbours, and being restricted in your ambitions. Although there is no immediate cure for the last of these, there are ways to overcome the other two.

Hiding the boundaries

Blurring a garden's boundaries immediately increases the sense of space. After all, there is nothing as efficient at defining space as fences and walls. This is why the developers of many modern housing estates do away with the strict demarcation of front gardens. If you can't clearly see where the garden ends, you won't be constantly reminded of its size.

Hide your boundaries with plants: swathe your walls and fences with climbers and wall shrubs, and fill any gaps at the base with low-level plants; position taller trees or shrubs so that they jut up over the fence line to soften its edge and create a varied skyline. Unless you are creating a hedge, avoid using plants that are all the same height, as this will just create a living boundary.

If your garden is big enough, consider incorporating a pergola, archway or pierced screen between the house and the far boundaries to interrupt your line of sight. Don't block the view altogether, since it is glimpses of the landscape beyond your plot that will increase the sense of space (*see* page 19). In a very tiny garden, positioning a trellis-framed arbour just a few feet from the outer boundaries and planting up the space in between will create the illusion that the space is much larger than it really is.

Here an espaliered hedge has been trained above a stone wall. This subtle boundary provides privacy while still allowing plenty of light through to the secluded seating area.

Infinity-edge pools

A popular trend with the designers of upmarket modern gardens, particularly in the USA, is the infinity-edge pool. The far edge of the pool is hidden from view, so it looks as though there is nothing holding the water in place. This sounds rather grand, but if the ground drops away beyond your garden leaving you with an open sky or a distant view, it might well be that you could recreate the effect on a smaller scale. The reflection of the sky in the water will enormously increase the sense of space.

Playing with perspective

In art, perspective gives depth to a scene depicted on a two-dimensional canvas, making it look as though it is in three dimensions. In gardens, which are already in three dimensions, perspective plays tricks with the size and appearance of objects in relation to each other when they're viewed from one particular point.

Whether deliberately considered or not, perspective has an effect in every garden. In well-designed gardens, it is often used to draw the line of sight towards a focal point or to confuse the eye by making the space seem longer, shorter, wider or narrower. It can also make specific objects within the garden seem larger or smaller.

Clever use of perspective can increase the feeling of space in a small area. Long, narrow pavers used widthways across a garden, or at an angle, will make it appear shorter, but much wider. On the other hand, a small but realistic statue at the end of a narrow path – or one that narrows as it goes away from you – will make the distance seem much greater, because our eyes want to believe the statue is life size.

Two paths that appear parallel but in reality get closer together will also give an illusion of length. Or you can even 'borrow' the landscape beyond the garden (*see* page 19), angling the paths so that they would converge at a focal point somewhere in the distance, thereby drawing the eye beyond the garden boundary.

Repeating objects or shapes – for example, rectangles of hard landscaping or grass – that have the same proportions but get progressively smaller as they are used further away is another trick garden designers use to increase the perceived size of the space, as your eyes will take them all to be the same size as the one nearest to you.

Narrow pavers laid crossways and emphasized with red lines make this space seem wider. The limited colour palette underscores the effect.

Parallel lines seem to converge as they go away from you, here focusing attention on the planted container.

Steps and a simple slate pillar create height in the corner of a garden. This feature also incorporates raised beds, which add another layer of interest.

Creating different levels

Adding to the number of horizontal planes in your garden is another way to increase the feeling of space (*see also* pages 41–3). From simple steps, columns and plinths to more complex verandas, decks and sunken areas, there are plenty of options. The way this works is that the eye is diverted by the many horizontal and vertical lines, along with the variations in light and shade, and cannot take in the whole space in one glance. Instead, your brain processes small areas one at a time, building up a picture of the garden. Varying the weight of the different elements will add to the interpretation work the brain has to

do. For example, instead of building a pergola with supports and cross-beams of equal weight, choose heavy beams that are supported by slender uprights, or have the beams cantilevered with only one set of uprights. The harder the brain has to work, the more interesting and substantial the garden will seem to the viewer.

Plinths of almost any size and material double up as seating (if the height is right) or display areas for containers or statues. Decking is a very versatile way to produce major changes of level, since the length of

the supporting legs can be altered to suit. If you don't have room for two decked seating areas, make large steps out of decking slabs or position them away from the main deck, linked with narrower walkways and planted areas.

Steps up or down to a small level area, or beside a raised pool, provide opportunities for planted containers, or you can fill raised beds with

Don't forget

Dividing a garden into smaller parts can create a sense of hidden space where none exists (see pages 22–3).

plants that will tumble down over the steps, softening their edges while accentuating their form. You might also incorporate a balustrade or simple handrail to provide interest without taking up much space.

Using lines and curves

Both straight and curved lines can help in your quest to make your space seem bigger. Use zigzags or curves for paths, border edges and hard landscaping; they create a flow through the garden and ensure that your eye takes longer to reach its destination. A straight path from the top to the bottom of your garden will immediately draw attention to its length, but if you blur its edges, angle the bricks or paving stones and give it a few very gentle curves, this will appear to lengthen it and so make the space it sits in seem larger.

If you're planning a paved patio, at the very least stagger the joints; better still, incorporate a subtle pattern just to provide a lift to the design and, again, prevent your brain from instantly 'understanding' the space. With decking, consider incorporating steps that are triangular in shape, rather than rectangular; these will soften the transition between the hard and the soft landscaping while avoiding a blocky look, which inevitably reduces the feeling of space.

Vertical lines are also effective. One of the best ways to improve a dull garden is to provide height in

the form of a pergola, an obelisk, an arch or an arbour (*see* pages 49–51). The vertical lines of structures like this give a visual change of pace and divert your eye up to the sky. Consider using diagonal lines too – they take you on quite a different trajectory, up and away from the limited space at ground level.

Borrowing the landscape

Borrowing the landscape is a simple idea that involves arranging your garden to give the impression that it extends into the landscape beyond its true limits. Done well, this can make your plot feel dramatically bigger without costing a penny or adding to the workload.

Take a look at what's visible beyond your boundaries. If there is a pleasant view, even just of the top of a tree, or perhaps an attractive building, try to organize elements

within your garden so that your eye is drawn along that vista. It takes a bit of care, but think about placing an archway, pergola or moon gate (a circular opening in a wall, fence or trellis) within the garden so that when you sit on your terrace or indoors, you look through it to glimpse the view beyond. Augment the effect by using materials and colours that echo those in the landscape you are borrowing.

If you're bordered by gardens that are heavily planted, position some of your plants so that they merge with those outside, making the two seem to belong together. You might even consider planting the same types of tree or shrub to complete the illusion. Line up your plants with those of your neighbours to suggest a continuous hedgerow, or group them to create the impression of a thicket or copse.

Curved and straight lines along with imaginative planting produce a sense of depth and space in this seating area.

Light shining onto the blue-painted wall at the far end of this exotic garden suggests that it extends way into the distance.

Lighting

Careful use of lighting to create splashes of brightness and long, mysterious shadows is an excellent way of giving the impression of space at night (*see also* pages 56–7). A spotlight positioned behind an old door that has been fixed close to a wall or fence will produce a glow, suggesting there is something intriguing behind the door. An old window frame glazed with stained glass or filled with an intricate metal grille could be used in a similar way. Lights that shine up through foliage give it a depth that is not apparent during the day. Make sure that the lights do not focus too heavily on your boundaries, since this will create just the feeling of claustrophobia that you want to avoid.

Using colour

Colour offers many opportunities to create or diminish space. Think of the blue-grey or purple tinge of far-off mountains. These colours can be used to reproduce the same sense of distance in your garden. Fences or walls painted in soft blues, lavenders or violets and delicate purples will seem much further away than those in rich or bright hues. In shady spots these colours can also absorb light, creating a rather sombre ambience where light is scarce – so tread carefully. Alternatively, use silvery browns or greys and pale olive greens. Like bluey greys, these natural shades recede into the background, but they also reflect some light, making them a better choice in shade.

In shallow borders, purple, blue and violet flowers and rich-coloured foliage produce a feeling of depth, especially if they're planted behind brighter colours in strong tones, like orange or yellow, which always seem to be much closer than they are. Be cautious with black or very dark foliage plants; these are best placed in front of pale colours, or they can appear as 'holes' in the design.

Using form

Along with colour, it's important to consider form. Small leaves, for example, will increase the idea of space simply because your eyes cannot focus on them all at once. Leaves in pale greens or silvery shades increase this effect. A clump of bamboo or ornamental grass swaying in the breeze seems almost immeasurably deep. At the opposite end of the scale, the large leaves of a banana (*Ensete* or *Musa*) or canna lily can make the garden seem larger, since it is obviously big enough to accommodate them. Combining forms so that small leaves are viewed through large ones creates an even greater sense of depth.

A few large plants sitting comfortably in a small area can have the effect of making the space seem bigger.

Sometimes, particularly in very small or very enclosed areas, it can be useful to use trickery to increase the feeling of space. Optical illusions are fun and can be very persuasive. Our brains are quite easy to fool, because when we look at something they use their experience of life to interpret it in the most logical fashion – and occasionally logic is not what is required. We can make use of this phenomenon in garden design.

Trompe l'oeil

The time-honoured way to confuse the brain is to use *trompe l'oeil* (meaning 'trick the eye'). This is usually done with painting, particularly murals, but may also use sculpture. Although often focused on the vertical plane, *trompe l'oeil* can also be used to create tricks with perspective on paving or other horizontal surfaces.

In gardens, popular *trompe l'oeil* themes are those that depict a believable scene that could belong to the garden – a door opening into a courtyard, perhaps, or a view of flower beds through an archway. The painting style needs to match the style of your outdoor space for the illusion to be effective. For example, in a formal garden, you could paint a view of a group of topiary box around a simple pool, or a row of pleached limes leading into the distance. In a cottage garden, a creaky gate (real or painted) could appear to lead to a shady bower with foxgloves and roses – some real ones planted to frame the painting will add to the impression of reality.

Reflection

Mirrors can create a very convincing illusion of space. When well positioned, their effect can be so confusing that you lose your sense of direction. One of the very simplest illusions is to place

The only limit to successful trickery is your imagination.

① These shutters lead nowhere. But who's to know?

② The reflection in this mirrored arch increases both the space and the amount of light in this dark corner.

③ Our eyes know that this is a painted landscape, yet it invokes a feeling of openness and distance.

a small mirror so that it is surrounded by plants in a quiet spot in the garden, so you just catch glimpses of its reflection out of the corner of your eye. Or you could go much further and clothe a whole wall or fence with an arcade of mirrors, separated by two-dimensional arches or trellis, so that it looks as though the garden

continues beyond them. The complete reflection will effectively double the garden's size.

Don't forget

Birds cannot tell the difference between reflection and reality. To avoid fatal collisions, site mirrors only in restricted spots, where they cannot fly at speed.

Creating privacy and seclusion

A secluded oasis of calm is one of the most precious things in any garden, whatever its size. Even when you get on perfectly well with the neighbours, there are times when you want to be able to pop outside to enjoy a quiet cup of coffee without everyone knowing what you're doing. One of your top priorities will be to create some private areas.

The conditions in your garden

The way you compose your secluded areas will be influenced by several factors: your garden's situation, where you are overlooked, whether you're exposed to extremes of weather, and whether you have a lovely view. A private area should always be somewhere you can sit in comfort, so it should be sheltered from strong winds but perhaps open to a gentle breeze. Ideally, it will offer some shade for hot days but still be sunny enough to be warm on cooler ones. Frequently it is easier to plan on two or more private areas, for different times of day, at different

A white wisteria makes a magnificent display on this pergola, providing shade, seclusion and height.

periods of the year, and in different kinds of weather.

Using plants

For the most simple and unobtrusive screening there is nothing to beat a selection of plants. Tall, slender, shrubby plants, such as Japanese maples (*Acer palmatum*) and snowy mespilus (*Amelanchier lamarckii*), or clump-forming bamboos and the taller grasses, can be positioned very precisely right beside your seating area to hide you from overlooking windows. The great thing about using plants near seating is that they give you something to look at, and maybe smell, while you sit, and the

Surrounded by a dense planting of bamboos, this sunny patio is a peaceful, secluded haven, shut away from the world.

Don't forget

Whether you want privacy or to hide a distant eyesore, the nearer you position a tree, arch or pergola to your seating area or viewpoint, the more effective a screen it will be.

breeze rustling their leaves is a pleasant and surprisingly effective distraction from nearby noise.

Using pergolas

A pergola is a straightforward way to create an enclosed space (*see* pages 49–51). An open structure of uprights and cross-beams, a pergola can form a covered walkway or a rectangular seating area. Either way, the structure itself can often be positioned carefully so that it also screens windows overlooking other parts of the garden. If you plan to use your pergola as a seating area, you may want to grow plants over it to increase the sense of seclusion. Alternatively, use coverings made of natural materials, such as trellis or bamboo screening, or perhaps a canopy made from sail fabric, to protect you from the odd shower.

If the pergola adjoins a house wall or a fence, one side will already be enclosed, and this may provide sufficient privacy. In a more exposed site, you may want to enclose three sides – perhaps by using a solid screen along the back and more lightweight ones on the other two sides. You can then sit well back inside on hot days but nearer the open side on cooler ones.

Using arbours

Arbours (*see* page 49) are intended to be covered with plants, which should ensure you can slip inside and remain unnoticed for as long as you wish. They can also be used as annexes to pergolas to increase the feeling of seclusion or to provide additional protection from wind.

Arbours provide the perfect peaceful sitting place for one – or, at most, two. As they are little more than covered benches, they can be slotted into quite small spaces. They also make great focal points and can help increase the sense of space, as well as direct your line of sight to other areas of interest. Some arbours incorporate storage space under the seat, making them all the more useful in a small garden.

Using screens and arches

Screens are extremely useful for providing privacy and seclusion in an understated way, especially early on in the garden's life, when the plants have not yet grown to fill their allotted space. The best way to divide a garden into smaller areas without being too heavy-handed, screens are available in a variety of designs and can be used for different effects (*see* pages 33–4). An open trelliswork screen loosely clothed with plants, for example, will create a semi-private area, while more solid screens made of rush, bamboo slats, bark strips or brushwood could be used to make an entirely hidden space for those times when you want to shut out the world.

Trelliswork panels are often fixed to either side of an arch of the same material, creating an attractive focal point as well as inviting you to enter the secluded garden 'room' beyond. Even freestanding arches (which always look better when 'anchored' by planting) will by virtue of their height provide a certain amount of screening when in the right place. For more on arches, *see* pages 49–50.

A delicately planted trellis provides an effective barrier against prying eyes without overpowering the seating area.

What's your style?

If you're going to design, construct and plant a whole small garden from scratch, it really is important to spend some time thinking about the garden styles that appeal to you most. The majority of recognized styles tend to be categorized as either 'informal' or 'formal', but there are endless interpretations and variations. Try to choose and stick to one main style, since this will make many decisions much more straightforward and should produce a pleasing and cohesive result.

In this cottage-style garden, the hard landscaping, including a weathered gate and fence, provides a sensitive framework for the ebullient plants.

Informal

The majority of gardens would probably fall under the banner of 'informal', since they have grown up on an *ad hoc* basis over many years without any particular design input. However, there are several distinct and recognizable informal styles, of which the cottage garden is probably the best known.

Cottage gardens

The cottage-garden style is traditional and very English. It is characterized by a hotchpotch of plants growing together – often vegetables alongside flowers. Cottage gardens usually contain a great mixture of flowering varieties from simple, old-fashioned lupins, foxgloves and delphiniums to more blowsy types such as dahlias and sweet peas. There are no rules in a cottage garden.

Prairie gardens

Less easy to achieve, particularly in limited spaces, prairie gardens are a decorative interpretation of the

Mixed pebbles and fossils create a seaside ambience. Grasses, colourful dahlias and large-leaved canna lilies add to the holiday atmosphere.

flower and grass combinations found in the American prairies. Sinuous lines and large spots of colour are typical, with a few specimen plants providing the permanent structure. Dense planting is essential. The design is often intended to be viewed as a whole, meaning it will not always be the best choice for fragmented gardens or awkward shapes.

Urban jungle

There are two challenges in creating an urban jungle: fitting in as many plants as possible and then keeping them alive through the winter. The emphasis is usually on foliage, with flowers coming second. Structural plants with large leaves or colourful stems form the basis of the 'jungle', with a thick underplanting of smaller specimens. Not all the plants have to be truly tropical. (*See* pages 74–5 for a jungle garden design.)

Seaside

You don't have to be on the coast to have a seaside garden. Decking, railway sleepers, pebbles, sand and heavy rope will create a coastal ambience, and carefully selected plants – such as tamarisk, sea holly, euphorbias, osteospermums and phormiums – do the rest.

Wildlife

With suitable plants and a sensitive gardening style, any garden will attract wildlife. However, gardens

This pretty garden contains a wide variety of flowering plants and plenty of nooks and crannies – which also make it an excellent wildlife haven.

Dense planting is the hallmark of an urban jungle. Here, the long, slender fronds of a tree fern tower over smaller grasses and ferns.

specifically created to be a wildlife haven will have natural ponds, beetle banks, stacks of sticks for nesting insects and plenty of bird boxes. The plants should appeal to butterflies and bees, and are chosen to provide a year-round supply of nectar and other food, as well as suitable accommodation for a variety of fauna (*see* page 98).

In this traditionally formal garden softly planted, decorative urns emphasize the strong, simple, horizontal and vertical lines that otherwise predominate.

Formal

Most of us think of grand stately homes – all box hedge and knot gardens – when we think of formal gardens, but in fact, the neat and restricted nature of the formal style makes it a perfect fit for a small urban garden. Formal gardens usually rely on a strong backdrop of evergreen plants, normally smartly clipped and shaped, accented with colour in a very selective and controlled way. They are often laid out in a geometric pattern, and frequently symmetrical. Restraint is key: this style is no good for those of us who make snap purchases at the garden centre.

If you like the idea but also want some flexibility in your design, consider incorporating a formal area into a generally more relaxed overall scheme. A couple of pieces of formal topiary, for example, will bring an air of control to an otherwise exuberantly planted garden.

Minimalist

The main aim of a minimalist garden is to produce an effect using very little – perhaps only a few plants, or maybe plenty of plants, but just very few different varieties. Minimalist spaces are usually calm and well considered, with each plant, container and piece of furniture playing a very particular part. This is why minimalist gardens come under the 'formal' heading, though sometimes they can be quite informal in nature. Minimalism is ideal for the very small urban

Don't forget

Don't feel intimidated or constrained by having to follow a pre-designed style. In the end, any good gardener with a reasonably artistic eye can create a style that is unique to that particular garden.

From the exactly placed stones to the bare-branched climber, each element of this minimalist garden is deliberately and beautifully counterbalanced.

A mixture of formal hedging and informal planting produces a vibrant and attractive courtyard garden. The effect may look casual but, as with the majority of successful gardens, it has been very carefully orchestrated.

Family gardens

A family garden can be made using any of the styles described, tailoring the design to its primary function as a family space (see also pages 72–3). In practice, this means allowing room for ball games and other child-orientated pastimes, not forgetting a place for them to garden, of course. Formal gardens are less easy to adapt for children, since football or bicycle damage will be harder to disguise, but you could create a formal area close to the house, with a less structured playing area beyond, or you may be able to indulge your formal side in the front garden (see pages 112–13), where the children are less likely to play.

Hard landscaping takes centre stage in this formal city garden. The walls seem to grow upwards, diverting attention from the restrictions of the space.

garden, particularly roof terraces and balconies, where too many different shapes and colours would make the space seem crowded.

Maintenance

Formal or informal, most densely planted gardens take some looking after. If you're looking for something that can be smartened up in an hour or two each week, opt for simple planting and plenty of largish containers. Avoid a lawn, since this takes time to keep looking good and use gravel, paving, brick or bark chippings for ground cover instead.

What's your shape?

Whatever the shape of your garden, you'll find that there are a number of ways to make the most of your space and create an interesting layout. It's amazing how you can completely alter the appearance and feel of a garden by dividing up the space differently, or by changing the shape or position of key elements such as the lawn or seating area. Here are some ideas for different effects that can be achieved using simple combinations of basic rectangles, squares and circles or part-circles.

Asymmetrical gardens

Irregular gardens, such as triangular plots, are often considered awkward, but there are some advantages. They can be easier to divide into separate areas than a regular shape, as you're not restricted by the idea of a formal rectangle or square, and you can make good use of an 'awkward' corner: it might make an ideal seating area or feature a focal point or, if screened off, could house a shed or bins. Countless terraced houses have a side passage 'tacked on' to the main garden. It needn't be dead space: there are ways to integrate it into the overall design. (*See also* pages 116–17.)

When a garden tapers to a point or a restricted corner, use bold shapes of differing sizes in the middle – like these interconnecting circles – to draw the eye away from the perimeter. Plenty of planting in the surrounding beds will hide awkward angles. Use arches or trellis to create separate 'rooms' in the middle space, or to lead to an odd corner, creating the illusion that a lot more garden lies beyond.

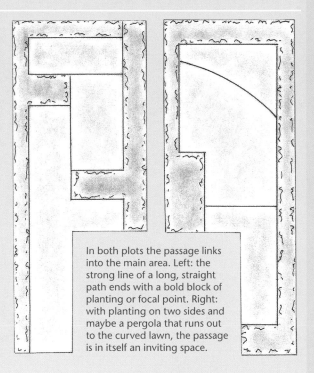

In both plots the passage links into the main area. Left: the strong line of a long, straight path ends with a bold block of planting or focal point. Right: with planting on two sides and maybe a pergola that runs out to the curved lawn, the passage is in itself an inviting space.

Short and wide gardens

With the bottom of the garden so close, you need to distract attention with features within the plot. Disguise all boundaries with planting, making use of any attractive views beyond, and use tall plants, structures and other features to give the illusion of greater depth.

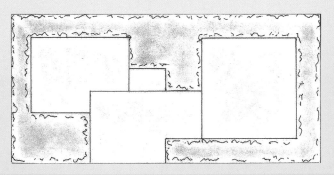

Irregular, interlocking shapes focus interest on the heart of the garden. Trees, tall plants and garden structures at either side, with low-level plants and focal points on the far boundary, will make the plot seem narrower. Paving or decking laid lengthways on the patio will help to elongate it.

Long and narrow gardens

It's best to avoid having borders running parallel with the walls or fences, as this will accentuate the garden's narrowness. Instead, you could divide the length into two or more 'rooms'. Making separate areas means you can create different types of garden within one: maybe a formal terrace, then a flower garden, followed by a children's play area, vegetable plot or wildlife garden. Divide these areas with planting, hard landscaping or structures to create subtle shifts or distinct boundaries. If the idea of rooms doesn't appeal, you can use visual 'tricks' to reduce the feeling of length. Use meandering curves or diagonals, which draw the eye across rather than down the length of the garden.

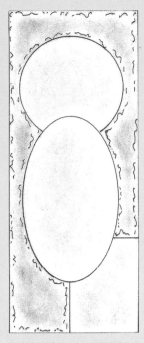

Two bold shapes, circular and oval, interlink to create softly curving borders. They vary in depth and there is a subtle shift of mood as one lawn leads to the other (possibly with a change of level) and a different style of planting.

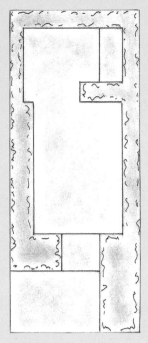

Rectangles are used to create three distinct 'rooms', divided with planting brought in from the sides. An arch over the path linking the patio and the main lawn would ensure the whole garden cannot be seen at once, inviting exploration.

Setting the open spaces on the diagonal takes the eye from side to side, making the plot feel wider. It also offers opportunities for plenty of points of interest along the journey to a patio tucked into the planting at the far end.

Square gardens

A square garden can have a rigid feel, so try to offset the predictability of the garden's outline: use bold shapes asymmetrically to create a fluid design, and think in three dimensions, varying heights and levels of features and planting, so there's always plenty of interest. A square shape readily lends itself to a formal design with geometric shapes in a symmetrical pattern, but an informal, less static layout can be a challenge.

A traditional design of the potager type is still pleasing. A modern interpretation, while retaining the formality of the layout, would use more contemporary planting. Add height in the centrepiece with a tree, obelisk or column.

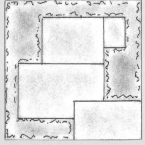

Square shapes are used asymmetrically to create a more flowing design; the patio is set off-centre. Trellis could be used to divide the areas and different levels could be created using raised beds, steps and decks.

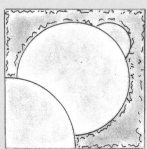

Circles create a more relaxed effect. From the patio the eye focuses on the longest dimensions (the diagonals), making the garden appear wider. A focal point opposite the patio and steps down to the lawn would add interest.

Garden elements and features

It's important that all the individual elements of a garden work together. Before you set your plans in stone, spend a bit of time considering the various items and materials that you want to use. Look at them individually and also think about how they will relate to each other and to your house; find ways to link structures, elements and features, so that they look comfortable with each other as well as within their surroundings.

Considering your options

Whether or not you already have a particular garden style in mind, you need to think carefully about what you would like in the way of specific elements such as paths, patios, fences, sheds and similar permanent features. These are all crucial to the final look and feel of your garden, and they are not inexpensive, so you need to be sure you've got them right.

Making choices

When it comes to these long-term elements, the options are just as numerous whether your garden is measured in metres or in acres. However, you will have your own particular needs, lifestyle and budget to take into account, and the Garden-planning checklist on page 63 will help you narrow the choices.

A good starting point is to take a wander down your road and see what other people have done. When you visit friends, take a good look at everything in their gardens – not just the planting. Once you start noticing what's under your feet,

Different materials can be used together with great success. Here, a slate patio is contrasted with white rendered walls and stone step treads and coping.

what's marking the boundaries, and what's supporting those beautiful plants, you begin to realize how much choice you have.

As soon as you know you're going to be making a new garden, or revamping your existing one, start looking through magazines and newspaper supplements, cut out photographs of gardens and garden elements that appeal to you, and begin to build up a 'storyboard'.

Try to visit a landscaping supplier: most display the various types of paving and timber products in ways that will give you a pretty good idea

of how they will look in reality. Your local garden centre will also have a selection of products, though the choice may be more limited.

You just have to weigh up all the pros and cons – and be prepared to change your mind a few times before making a final decision.

Don't forget

Manufacturers of landscaping products produce annual catalogues with excellent photographs showing ways in which their materials can be used in real garden situations. Ask your local landscaping and building suppliers for copies or order them online.

Flower shows

It's well worth trying to get to at least one of the annual RHS flower shows. Look carefully at the hard landscaping materials and the decorative features, not only in the show gardens created by professional garden designers but also in the displays put on by manufacturers and craftsmen. The Chelsea Flower Show in London gets the most publicity, but there are also RHS shows at Hampton Court Palace, Cardiff, Malvern and Tatton Park, in Cheshire. Just remember to take your notebook!

Walls, fences, screens and hedges

When they are used as boundary markers, walls, fences and hedges are perhaps the most important elements in a garden, since they enclose and define your space. They are usually fairly permanent structures, intended to create privacy, discourage intruders and form the basic structure within which everything else presides. Within the garden, they are used as dividers or screens, and are particularly valuable in a small space. Used to increase intimacy and interest, they are usually more subtle and ephemeral, and their style can be more quirky.

A rendered wall painted a light colour keeps your attention within the garden enclosure and provides a simple backdrop for the planting.

Walls

Walls are generally used to create a boundary, but they can also be erected to divide areas of the garden or to act as retaining walls for banks, terracing and raised beds (*see* pages 41–3). A brick boundary wall is almost certainly going to be more expensive than a fence or hedge to install and to maintain, but when well built and cared for it will look good for many years to come.

Existing walls

If you've inherited beautiful, well-maintained brick walls around your garden or courtyard, you're extremely fortunate. The warm, mellow colours of old bricks create a lovely backdrop for most plants, and also combine happily with most other hard landscaping materials,

including wood, stone and concrete. However, in many old properties the boundary walls are in a bad state of repair and, at the very least, need repointing. Sometimes it will look better if they are then painted. It's amazing how much a coat of white paint can lighten up a wall in a basement or shady courtyard. Alternatively, you could paint them a rich, deep colour for dramatic effect.

Practical pros and cons

Walls trap heat, which makes them excellent surrounds for seating areas on summer evenings and for protecting warmth-loving climbers and wall shrubs (*see* pages 92–6). However, high walls may cast heavy shade and the rain-shadow side can be very dry, particularly as wall foundations tend to suck up water (*see* page 60).

New walls

In some new-build properties you have the chance to choose what type of boundary marker to put in. If you're planning on staying there for a long time, the expense of brick walling may well be worth it. You won't regret your choice.

For freestanding walls that are going to act as features or dividers within a garden, it is cheaper to use concrete blocks and render them.

Don't forget

The deeds of your property may indicate, in writing or with a T-mark on the plan, the boundary for which you are responsible. An H-mark means responsibility is shared. If there is no information in the deeds, you may have to rely on the Seller's Property Information Form. Sometimes the pattern of ownership along the same side of the street is a guide.

The result can be very effective. If the render is attractive, you can leave it as it is, otherwise paint it – maybe a pale neutral colour or a striking terracotta or deep red. A low dividing wall can double up as a seat and, with a hinged or removable top, storage (*see* page 46).

Always check with the local council to see if you need permission before putting up a new wall.

What style?

Depending on their style, walls can suit both formal and informal gardens. Half-height boundary walls can be topped with elegant ironwork panels or wood fencing for a smart, traditional look. In a rural setting, some of the most attractive brick walls have insets of flint or stone, particularly where these are the local material. Dry-stone walls are most suitable for cottage gardens, but with a smooth-cut or polished coping they will also look good in a more sophisticated rural garden.

Fences

Where there are no existing boundary markers, fencing is the cheapest and quickest option. Good quality, pressure-treated fencing is fairly long-lasting and can be coloured and preserved with wood paint or stain. It is relatively quick to install, and fencing panels come in a range of heights and standard panel widths, making it easy to replace

broken sections. Fences make an excellent backdrop for plants as well as a sturdy support for climbers. They take up minimal space and can be unobtrusive or a design feature in their own right (*see* page 35).

Trellis attached to a wall or fence is extremely useful where the surface beneath is unattractive, enabling you to conceal and soften the boundary with climbers and wall shrubs. It is particularly valuable in a small garden, because you can fit in more plants.

Screens

Screens are not sturdy enough for creating boundaries, but they are excellent for dividing the garden into different areas. They're cheap, easy to install and take up very little space, and are available in a variety of heights; their lightweight nature means that even the tallest models will not look too dominant. Screens also make a great foil for plants. Their downside is that some of the more decorative models are not very long-lasting.

Don't forget

Invariably, the most satisfying hard landscaping for your garden will echo the materials used to build your home. This follows the basic design principle of unity (see page 10).

Although lovely, the brick wall around this garden was not high enough. Wooden lattice fencing panels have provided privacy and are attractive too.

Painted a rich shade of burgundy, this traditional-style trellis screen creates a classy divider.

A bamboo screen looks wonderful beside a bamboo plant, underlining the jungle theme.

Hedges can be any height you wish, but you will need to keep them regularly trimmed.

Different types of screens can produce very different effects. Probably the most popular is trellis, which is very versatile and suits all types of gardens. It comes in various shapes and sizes and can be painted to blend in or stand out. It makes an excellent frame for plants and is about the only screen that is entirely see-through, while giving the impression of solidity. Very resilient, it can last at least ten years.

Willow-weave has a rustic look but can work well in an urban design as a backdrop for architectural planting in galvanized containers. Brushwood screens are ideal for rural gardens, where they may be swagged with roses and clematis. In a minimalist or jungle garden, you could use bamboo, whereas reed fits a seaside theme.

Hedges

Like walls, hedges make excellent boundaries and dividers, and are long-lasting. They are inexpensive to put in, make effective windbreaks and are a good background for plants, while also creating a habitat for all sorts of wildlife. Birds love them. You can grow hedges to be any size, from knee-high dividers up to 2m (6½ft), above which they can be classified as a nuisance to your neighbours. (*See also* page 89.)

On the downside, hedges take a while to reach the desired size – ten years or more, depending on what

Pleached hornbeams make a good 'hedge on stilts', ideal for a small garden as they aren't greedy for space at ground level.

height you want. They are space-hungry, growing up to 1m (40in) deep, and need cutting twice a year. Hedges can dry the soil, especially on the rain-shadow side, and create dense shade, making it difficult to grow plants close to them, which is not ideal in a very small garden. While it is establishing, a hedge will not provide much privacy and will be no good at deterring unwanted visitors, so you may want to put up a temporary brushwood screen or bamboo panel. Once it is mature, however, it will provide as much seclusion as you could wish.

A 'hedge on stilts' (*see* left) makes a very striking, if pricey, feature for a small garden. With the growth trained on a framework, it provides screening above head height with an unimpeded view through the tree trunks below.

Boundary fences

In recent years there has been an explosion of styles in boundary fencing for gardens. This might have made choosing a fence more fun, but it can be difficult to reach a final decision. It boils down to two main considerations: the look you want to achieve and, as always, the cost.

Timber panels

Traditional shiplap and close-board panels (often of feathered-edge planks) are very widely available and usually reasonably priced. They do a good job without being fussy or intrusive. The smartest panels are made of precision-sawn planks, attached to horizontal wooden rails (arris rails).

There are many variations in fencing styles, for example panels where lateral, vertical or diagonal planks are alternated either side of their supports ('hit and miss'), or those where a small gap is left between each, which are less solid but more wind resistant.

A popular option is to use solid panels to about 1.2m (4ft), and then to have wooden trellis 30cm (12in) or so high on top. This reduces the shadow the fence casts without overly reducing privacy. Trellis panels come in a range of designs. For added security, metal 'railing toppers' can be fitted instead.

Strips of battening fixed laterally have been used to enclose this space, providing privacy as well as making the area seem larger than it is.

Finishing touches should include a coping to protect the fence from the weather, particularly rain, and finials can be fitted to the post tops.

There are various openwork fences, including post-and-rail and palisade (sometimes called picket). These mark boundaries without obscuring views, but don't offer screening and may not prevent children getting out.

Bespoke options

You don't have to buy fences off the peg. One of the simplest ways to make a fence is to attach 5 x 2.5cm (2 x 1in) timber battens horizontally, at intervals of 2.5cm (1in), to upright posts (see above). This can be used above an existing half-height wall. Vertical battens take the eye upwards, rather than along the length of the garden. Alternatively, you could have fun making a fence with pieces of timber or metal, using chunky logs (see below) or lengths of scaffolding pole, set vertically and close together, in concrete. These may be of varying heights for added interest, and can be painted or left untreated.

Don't forget

For a subtle design effect, stagger the height of the fence. This also reduces its visual impact. Use regular height changes to avoid the overall effect looking haphazard.

Don't feel you have to stick with standard fencing. Add personal touches or come up with your own designs.

① Trellis panels add height and interest on top of a shiplap fence.

② Half-poles set at different heights make an unusual but attractive screen.

③ Alternating planks soften the impact of this tall fence, as does the blue paint.

Surfaces underfoot

While the vertical boundary markers define your garden's space, much of its style is dictated by the horizontal surfaces you create within it. Your choice of materials also has an impact on the way that you use the garden and how comfortable, convenient and inviting it is to move through. You can combine different surfaces successfully in moderation, but always remember the principles of unity and harmony (*see* page 10) and consider their effect on the garden as a whole.

Lawns and other plants

Unless your garden is really tiny, don't discount having a lawn: grass is pleasing, relaxing and naturalistic. In city gardens, surrounded by buildings, grass brings a sense of stillness. However, if your garden is too small or the conditions are just not good enough for grass to thrive, don't despair. A carpet of ground-cover plants can be just as pleasing.

Soft to walk on and restful to look at, grass is unbeatable as a surface for certain parts of the garden. However, it does require regular maintenance.

Grass

Ideally, a lawn needs to be large enough to turn the lawnmower comfortably. Don't forget you need somewhere to store the mower and a compost bin for the grass cuttings.

The problem with lawns in small gardens is that they're often overshadowed by trees or buildings and all too soon grass gives way to moss and algae. If the shade is not too dense and you're making a new lawn, buy turf or a blend of seed that tolerates low light levels and be prepared to nurture your sward to keep it lush and healthy. If you have dense shade and are considering a lawn or are already looking at grass that is clearly not happy, you could try thinning overhead branches to increase light, but realistically a better option is an area of ground-cover planting.

Ground-cover planting

Creeping ground-cover plants are a lovely alternative to grass for small areas and are also excellent at softening the look of a big expanse

Low-growing plants, including thyme and thrift, look wonderful spreading across a path and help to integrate different paving materials.

of paving. Many of these plants also thrive in gravel and are aromatic, making them perfect for a seating area. You could create a stepping-stone path through drifts of plants to avoid treading on them, although some plants tolerate occasionally being walked on: thyme, for example, releases its lovely fragrance. In a sunny spot, try aubretias, California poppies (*Eschscholzia*), chamomile, small hebes, dwarf pinks (*Dianthus*) and sempervivums. For light shade you could use bugle (*Ajuga reptans*), lady's mantle (*Alchemilla mollis*) and Corsican mint (*Mentha requienii*). None of these can be stepped on regularly though.

Loose materials

The main types of loose surfacing materials used in gardens are gravel, pebbles and bark. These are mostly cheap and are easy to use, and fit into almost any shape, but they are a better choice for paths than for seating areas, since they do not guarantee a stable surface. Lay landscaping fabric underneath (a lightweight, semi-permeable sheet that helps to prevent weed growth) and peg it down to prevent any movement. Always put a greater depth of loose materials than you think you need (at least 5cm/2in); gravel and bark tend to disappear, some of it carried onto the lawn and into the house on your feet.

Gravel and pebbles

Gravel comes in a range of colours, shapes and sizes. The larger the size, the less likely you are to pick it up on your shoes. It looks perfect in formal and informal gardens and is particularly good for driveways and paths. It can be combined with bricks, paving slabs or sleepers, or used on its own. Carefully raked into neat patterns, it is the basis for many contemplative gardens.

Usually slightly larger than gravel, pebbles are used as decorative additions rather than for any large areas of hard landscaping. However, they can be set into concrete to make paths and informal surfaces.

Bark

Bark is usually dark and soft-textured and the perfect material for hidden paths at the backs of borders or through shrubs and trees. It will gradually rot away, and it is not hardwearing enough for well-used paths or patios. If you're planning a wildlife garden, bark is a good choice, and it makes a useful mulch.

Paving

Paving can be fitted into the tiniest of corners and along the narrowest of passages, and is suitable for paths, patios and steps (see page 43). At one end of the scale, you can opt for no-frills concrete squares, while at the other you can choose Italian marble or York stone pavers, which are very beautiful and very pricey. In the middle there's concrete and reconstituted stone cleverly made to look like real stone.

Rough-textured and real or imitation stone give a traditional feeling, especially if pavers are laid randomly or in staggered lines, or edged with brick or stone. For a modern look, lay large, smooth pavers or polished stone in simple geometric shapes. Square tiles in warm, rich ochres and hexagonal or lozenge shapes will look good on a patio, but are less easy to use successfully for pathways because the unusual shapes can seem fussy.

The texture and colour of this gravel area is perfect for the formally shaped plants and matching domes.

For a soft, informal surface, bark is a good choice. Here, it is kept in place with wooden planks.

Don't forget

Check before you buy real stone that the supplier is a member of an organization that works to ensure ethical trading.

This decorative paving with gravel inset is a clever way to lead your eye along a path to the plants.

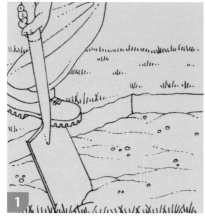

1

Use pegs and string to mark out the area to be paved, then dig out the soil to a depth of about 20cm (8in) below the intended surface level using a spade. Don't disturb the soil below that. If the paving butts right up to the wall of the house, the finished surface should be at least 15cm (6in) below the existing damp-proof course, and sloping slightly away from the house.

2

When the shape is right, knock some levelling pegs into the ground, using a plank and a spirit level to check that they are at the right height – about 10cm (4in) below your intended surface level (the depth of the slab plus a mortar bed of 50–60mm (2–2½in). Then spread an even layer of scalpings across the area and use a powered compactor plate (available to hire) to firm it level with the pegs.

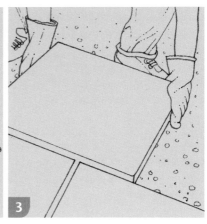

3

Lay out the slabs 'dry', in your chosen pattern, to check the fit and the look. It's well worth doing a paving plan (on paper or on the computer) in advance, as it's difficult to put mistakes right once the mortar has set. Aim for a gap of 10mm (½in) between slabs. Make sure the edges align, slightly adjusting the width of the joints between slabs, if necessary, to achieve this.

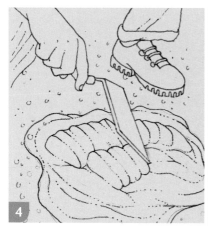

4

Mix the mortar, using a sloppy mix of 4:2:1 sharp sand : builder's sand : cement. A small barrow-load at a time should be about the right quantity to mix so you can use it up before it sets. Lay slabs a few at a time, setting them to one side while you spread the mortar. The mortar layer should be about 50–60mm (2–2½in) deep. Use a trowel to make a ridged surface, which will help with levelling the slabs.

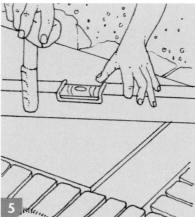

5

Carefully lift the first paving slab into position. Rest it on the mortar bed and gently tap it level with the handle of a hammer. Check with a spirit level to make sure you've kept an even, very slight slope away from the house wall. Repeat with the other slabs. Don't walk on the slabs for at least 24 hours so the mortar can set properly. Over-eagerness can result in uneven paving.

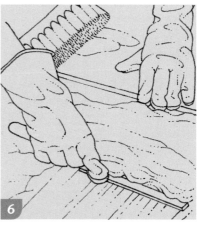

6

Slightly dampen the grouting mix (a dry mix of 3:1 builder's sand : cement) and use it to fill the joints, pushing it in with a gloved hand and leaving no gaps or cracks. Finish the joints with a raking or pointing tool to give a neat finish and sweep up any surplus mixture promptly. The grouting mix will gradually absorb water from the ground and from rainfall, and will then set hard.

Light and warm colours hint at Mediterranean climes; dark and cool ones are more formal. Choose your colour carefully: bright or white paving can be dazzling on a sunny day, while black or grey looks bleak in rain or in the dead of winter.

Brick and setts

Like paving, brick and other small-scale surfacing materials come in a range of designs and colours and are suitable for paths and seating areas. They are more time-consuming to lay, since each unit is small, but it is possible to purchase larger slabs made to look like a collection of bricks, setts or even lengths of wood to get a similar effect for less effort. You can spend a little or a lot, depending on whether you choose real granite setts or a realistic reproduction, genuine terracotta tiles or a modern version. You may be able to find reclaimed bricks, but take care: if they were originally made for walling, they may absorb water and crack in icy weather, or grow algae and become slippery when wet.

Bricks and setts can create any kind of ambience you want: country or town, modern or olde worlde. Smart, sharp-edged layouts tend to complement the most minimalist or formal designs, while older bricks in a looser pattern slip effortlessly into a cottage, seaside or jungle garden.

Because of their small size, bricks lend themselves to inventive patterns, such as circles and squares.

Brick and paving patterns

Depending on how you lay your bricks or slabs, you can create a variety of effects. Pick your pattern to make the most of your space.

Looking across a herringbone layout of bricks in the direction of the zigzag shortens and widens the area; looking along the zigzag lengthens and narrows it. A pathway of bricks laid lengthways looks much longer than one in which they are laid crossways.

Paving can be laid with the joints (courses) matching or staggered. Matching courses make a bold pattern, suitable for a modern or formal garden. Staggered joints are softer on the eye and foreshorten the distance across them. Laying paving crossways, so it becomes diamonds with triangular inserts, increases the feeling of space.

Natural stone flags (and their imitations) come in a variety of different-sized rectangles and squares, and are usually laid in a seemingly irregular way, called a 'random' pattern. The subtle effect is most suitable for informal styles of garden.

Choose a style that will suit your particular space.

① Herringbone makes a classic, formal pattern.

② Parquet is ideal for small areas.

③ Latticework makes use of half-bricks as well as whole ones.

④ Natural stone paving slabs are usually laid in 'random' patterns.

Softening the effect

For a relaxed feel, or if you just want to create more room for plants, leave out a few pavers and make a mini gravel bed. Allowing pretty, low-growing plants like *Erigeron karvinskianus* (above) to self-seed in cracks in paving, paths and steps has a softening effect too, and links these areas to the rest of the planting.

A walkway links the decking terrace with the garden in this small space, introducing an interesting change of materials and levels.

enhance the feeling of being beside the sea, add thick rope balustrades. Alternatively, you could aim for a tree-house effect or an exotic hide away, clothing the perimeters with trees and shrubs, or even building around existing planting for instant effect. If your garden overlooks a beautiful piece of countryside, use a deck like a viewing platform, 'borrowing' the landscape to extend your garden (see page 19).

Being materialistic

Wood is the main material used in decking, but this can be augmented with glass or metal detailing to produce different overall effects, from sleek and modern to highly decorative or traditional. The planks can be laid lengthways, crossways or diagonally, or even in smaller units reminiscent of parquet flooring – diagonal boards can help to create a sense of space. The timber can be painted or left to grow old gracefully.

Decking

Decking is relatively inexpensive, quick to erect and suitable for a wide range of sites, from flat to sloping, or where the ground is very uneven or drops away suddenly. Just remember that it is not a good idea in wet or shady places, as the wood will become slippery and rot. Unlike paving, if you want to change it at a later date, it is neither difficult nor expensive to remove.

You can make all sorts of different structures using basic decking modules: a freestanding seating area; an open veranda or a balcony; a set of wide steps; or a series of platforms to link the garden with the

house. Decks can be semi-enclosed with a balustrade or fully enclosed with a pergola or even a roof. You can use decking to create an atmosphere in a themed garden, for example a jungle garden (see pages 74–5) or a seaside garden. To

Bridges

Although they need careful use to avoid looking twee, bridges can be very attractive and can also create subtle changes of level in a garden. For instance, a small bridge positioned along a path and ideally over a dip in the ground or an area of water would add a focal point as well as a change in level. It can also provide the setting for some themed planting, such as bog plants or lush foliage plants.

Boardwalks

For a simple but effective use of decking, you might consider a raised walkway, which can be used for fun or have a distinct purpose. Where the garden drops away from the house, a decking walkway could act as a link between the two, perhaps jutting out into the garden like a jetty or meandering out like a boardwalk above marshy ground or through woodland.

Don't forget

Before you buy timber, check it comes from a responsibly managed source. Look out for the FSC label, which indicates it is approved by the Forestry Stewardship Council.

Terracing, raised beds and steps

The surfaces in a garden might define its style, but it is the changes in level that make it interesting, creating a better sense of the space and giving it a third dimension. An instant way to achieve height – so important in a garden – is to introduce different levels, even if your plot is naturally flat. They can be as simple or as complicated as you wish.

Terracing

A good way to introduce changes of level is with terracing. If your garden is very steep, the outlay can be worth every penny, making the space user-friendly from the top to the bottom. Even a slight slope converted into two or three terraces can be a great improvement, providing flat areas for seating, planting and grass. If possible, opt for fewer, larger terraces rather than many small ones: they will look better and allow a greater variety of plants. Just be careful if the slope goes upwards from your house – make sure that the terracing walls are not so tall that they seem to loom over you. Well-planned planting at the top and bottom can help to avoid this effect.

Style and substance

Terraces can be made with bricks, rendered concrete blocks, railway sleepers, large stones or gabions – mesh cages filled with stones. In many ways, terraces are like very large steps (*see* page 43), and can be built in similar styles with similar effects, but since they hold back soil from the upper level, they are best constructed by a professional.

Because of their larger size, the material used and their design will have a big impact on the overall feel of the garden. A series of terraces enclosed by brick walls will make the garden look very much under

Terracing this gentle slope has allowed the gardener to plant a range of drought-tolerant plants and create a pleasant seating area at its base.

Raised beds

Raised beds make life easier for gardeners with physical restrictions, but they are equally useful for those without. Where there is no need or scope for terracing, they can create changes of level combined with opportunities for planting. Because raised beds automatically increase plant height, shorter plants can fulfil a taller role. For example, where you have no space for a tree, a shrub in a raised bed can provide that essential third dimension – height – instead. They are also great if your soil is very poor or if you want to grow plants that need a particular soil type, for example plants that require acid soil. They can be made watertight to create pools, too (*see* pages 68–9 and 119).

Shapes and spaces

There is no need for you to make your raised beds the standard, utilitarian rectangle. Experiment to find what looks best in your space and design – circles, triangles, crescents and hexagons are all possibilities. While wide beds are probably easier to plant, narrow beds in sinuous curves could double up as garden dividers and make a wonderful place for alpines and rock plants. Nor do you have to make them a certain height. Low-level raised beds are less conspicuous, while higher ones can create secluded areas or increase shelter in exposed spots. Link higher and lower beds for a gentle rhythmic flow through the garden; set at the right heights, these raised beds could also double up as seating and eating spots.

Although these steps lead nowhere, they provide a subtle change of level in the corner of a tiny garden and soften the walls of the raised bed.

Gravel infill

Sloping drainage pipe

Footing

Weep hole

Retaining walls need to be built on a firm concrete footing and must be strong enough to keep back the soil. Gravel, drainpipes and drainage holes allow water to pass through.

control, while a couple of courses made with large pieces of local stone will seem completely natural. Where price is an issue, recycled, untreated sleepers are probably the cheapest choice and suit a wide range of styles from modern town gardens to seaside or country ones. With their combination of stone and metal, exposed gabions create an ultra-modern look. They can also be carefully planted to blend in where the main task is retaining soil. Walls made of concrete blocks can be faced with stone or rendered.

Steps

In a small space, steps can be used for seating and as a place to display plants in pots, not just a way of bridging levels. Steps can be made from many different materials – even railway sleepers and log rolls – or cut into a slope and covered with grass. However, the most common option is to build brick risers and top them with pavers for the treads.

Shape and size

Steps can be wide or narrow with deep or shallow treads; they can have straight edges (or noses) for a formal, no-nonsense feel or curved ones for a more relaxed effect. They can perform a key role in your garden design or merely suggest something very subtly. For example, a wide and deep flight of low steps can stretch out across a shallow slope, almost inconspicuous yet providing a reminder that this garden is not flat; on the other hand, short and narrow steps look like they're leading to somewhere important and maybe even rather secret. A gentle curve or changes of direction will increase this feeling. A straight flight of steps looks purposeful, even if it leads only to the back door, while a long, curved flight could be used at the end of the garden to give the impression that it flows on into another space, when really it just goes behind some shrubs to the dustbins. Ideally, risers should be no more than 10–15cm (4–6in) high and the treads at least 30cm (12in) from front to back.

In some cases you need handrails for safety reasons, but don't overlook their contribution to the overall design, and make sure they fit in with your garden style. Balustrades, too, can alter the feel of steps or a patio. A simple wooden handrail could double up as the frame for some low-level climbers or a support for hanging baskets. Decorative metal railings will introduce an air of sophistication, while a balustrade made of brick or stone creates more potential for planters and other decorative elements.

HOW TO make steps

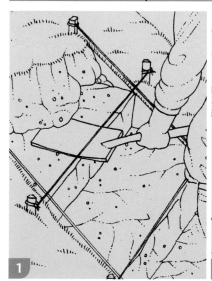

1 Use string and wooden pegs to mark out the position of the steps and the front of each tread. Make sure that the height of the risers and depth of the treads correspond to the materials you plan to use, such as bricks and paving stones. Using a spade, dig out the shapes of the steps in the soil. Compact the soil.

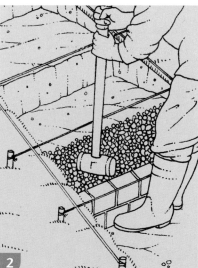

2 Starting at the bottom of the flight, make a concrete footing (*see* opposite) to ensure the steps will be level and don't collapse. Allow this to set before laying the brick courses to make the first riser. Check its alignment using a spirit level. When the riser has set, fill the area behind with well-compacted hardcore until it is level.

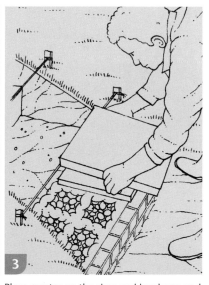

3 Place mortar on the riser and hardcore and position the tread. Construct the next riser at the back of the tread. Continue in this way until the final tread is flush with the surface at the top, then brush grouting mix (*see* Step 6, page 38) between the paving stones. Refill gaps around the edges of the steps with soil (you can turf or plant it later).

Water in small gardens

All gardens will benefit from a water feature in some form or another. Water's reflective qualities and its continuous, gentle movement bring a space to life, while also instilling a sense of calm. An area of water makes a very simple focal point, and the background sound of running water is surprisingly effective at muffling noise from outside the garden.

A plain water tank with a wall-mounted water spout looks entirely fitting in this simple outdoor space.

Space-saving water features

Bubble fountains, letterbox-style 'waterfalls' and wall-mounted water spouts are just a few of the smallest water features available. Some, such as Japanese deer scarers, have moving parts for added interest. It is amazing how long they can entrance you, and the sound of the water can be wonderfully soothing. Many are supplied complete with the necessary pump, and it is just a matter of installing them in an appropriate spot. Their biggest disadvantage is that they need an outdoor electricity supply – and outdoor electrics must be wired in by a professional – so bear this in mind when deciding where to place them.

If you don't want to go to the expense and trouble of electrics, consider a birdbath or container pool instead. Birdbaths can be tucked in among plants – where birds will appreciate them most – or used as an attractive feature or focal point.

HOW TO make a half-barrel pond

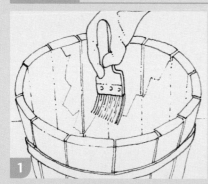

1 Scrape off any loose wood at the bottom of the barrel. Coat the inside of the barrel with pond paint using a paint brush. Leave the paint to dry, then do another coat. Place the barrel in its final position – you could partially bury it or stand it on the ground. Half fill the barrel with water using a hose.

2 Plant deep-water plants, marginal plants and submerged oxygenators in mesh aquatic baskets: line the baskets with hessian, fill with aquatic compost, insert the plant or plants into the compost and top-dress with a layer of grit or gravel, approximately 2.5cm (1in) deep.

3 Place deep-water plants at the pond base, then create 'shelves' for a couple more submerged plants by stacking one or more bricks to suit their planting depths. Set the planted baskets on the bricks. Top up the barrel with water if necessary. Finally, add floating plants, but avoid overcrowding.

Container pools can be made from any waterproof container, large or small, including suitably treated raised beds or half-barrels, although larger ones are easier to keep clean and grow plants in. Small volumes of water tend to overheat in summer and freeze too easily in winter. Site small container pools on or near the patio so that you can appreciate them close up.

Formal ponds

A formal pond usually has distinct edges constructed of stone, brick or blocks. It can stand above the ground or be sunk into it, but it is normally a geometric shape, such as a square, rectangle or circle. Where you have the space, you could group several ponds of different heights, but make sure you can reach them all for maintenance. Make a formal pond a key feature: put it centre stage and ensure it looks beautiful from all angles. If you don't want it to dominate the whole garden, consider tucking it into a screened-off space, where it can still play the leading role, but on a smaller stage.

Don't forget

Water and young children do not mix. Consider delaying installing a pond until they are older and opt for a feature that can be fitted with a metal grid on top covered with pebbles.

Practical considerations

Think about the supply of water and, usually, electricity to power a pump early on in your plans. It is important that they are conveniently located but also hidden: the last thing you want is to be able to see the hosepipe or cables running to your 'natural' stream. On balconies and roof gardens, the weight of water is an important consideration. You may need to check things out with a builder.

Although they are often simply bodies of water, formal pools may be planted, and water lilies (*Nymphaea alba* or *Nuphar lutea*) are the traditional choice. A fountain can also enhance the overall effect: choose a simple jet or a trickle waterfall for a modern pool; in a country setting, a spouting statue might look in keeping.

Natural pools

Unlike a formal pond, a natural one should look as if it has always been there and that the garden has grown up around it, so it is better off-centre and perhaps partially hidden from view. The edges should be shallow and the margins between water and land blurred, preferably with plants of all types filling the space and getting their feet wet. Loose pebbles or stones can

define the sloping banks, although decking is perfect for this job, too, and can provide a seating area and subtle focal point.

A gentle trickle of water or a pump set to bubble quietly will move and aerate the water, which is better for the inhabiting creatures.

Streams and rills

Rills or streams take quite a bit of work and expense to install, but there is no doubting their attraction. A rill usually consists of a formal canal of water, sometimes with little falls, and can even be made on the flat, while a stream is more natural and really needs a gentle slope to be convincing. When the pump is not running, the stream still needs to be full of water, and the design must take this into account.

Whether small or large, water features make a valuable contribution to the garden.

① This formal pond adds height and interest to an attractive seating area.

② A tiny bubble fountain can be slipped into the smallest of spaces.

③ A narrow rill creates a cool, attractive feature.

Storage and utility areas

When planning your garden, put storage and utility areas high on your list of priorities. It's important to consider them early on and make sure that they'll answer your needs as well as fit in with all your other plans for the garden. Although a bit dull, they are necessary, and if you make them convenient to use they will enable you to enjoy the rest of the garden while freeing up storage space in the house.

These unobtrusive storage units double up as seating and fit neatly into a space beside a raised bed.

Sheds and greenhouses

While there are upmarket wooden sheds, the most common ones, with shiplap walls and a felted roof, do the job equally well and are fairly inexpensive and long-lasting. They come in a range of sizes, with or without windows, and a coat of paint soon makes them fit in with your colour scheme.

The keener you become on gardening, the more useful you will find a greenhouse. Some so-called potting sheds are half-glazed on one side and could double up for storage and growing plants; otherwise, there are good-quality mini-greenhouses designed for even the smallest gardens. Available either as lean-tos or freestanding, these are made of glass and stainless steel and provide plenty of growing space.

Bins and recycling units

There are a few lean-to and low-level storage units on the market designed to take a wheelie bin or two – some are a lot more attractive than others. If you can afford it, it's worth getting something custom-built to fit into a particular space in the garden and to be sure that it suits your specific needs. Alternatively, use screens to disguise the bin area or put it behind the shed out of sight.

Green waste and water

Even a small garden will produce green waste and, together with what comes out of the kitchen, this can be used to create compost to improve your soil. If you haven't got room for a compost bin, try a wormery, which will fit into a tiny space. You need to buy the worms to go in them (usually from the same supplier) and these quickly create compost from your kitchen waste.

A water butt or two is a must, even in the smallest garden. All types of designs for restricted spaces are available and the best make attractive features in their own right.

Washing lines

Washing lines don't have to take up much room. Rotary dryers (also known as whirligigs) are probably the most efficient and can be stored when not in use. For a minute space, a retractable line is more sensible and easy to hide.

Nestled in a seaside-style garden, this little shed has been painted and now plays the role of a beach hut.

This custom-built wheelie-bin store has space for recycling boxes and is topped with a green roof.

One way to increase the decorative value of a utilitarian structure, such as a shed or garage, is to grow plants on its roof. So-called green roofs are growing in popularity and are particularly useful where space is at a premium, allowing you to have some additional greenery without losing precious outdoor room. You may need to make some structural alterations before installing one, but the outlay will be outweighed by the advantages.

Benefits of a green roof

A green roof provides a habitat for a range of insects, which in turn feed birds and other small creatures. In addition, green roofs absorb rainfall, releasing the water slowly and so reducing its impact on local drains and cutting the risk of flooding. The thick vegetation also insulates the building underneath, keeping it cool in hot weather and warm when it's cold.

The plants on top

Most domestic green roofs are planted with sedums. These are spreading, mat-forming succulents with pretty leaves in a range of shapes and colours, including reds, greys and blue-greens. When they flower, their blooms may be carried on long, slender stems or they simply dot the surface of the plant. Small and usually yellow, pink or white, they attract a variety of insects, including butterflies, bees and beetles. Sedums are most commonly used because they can survive in very little soil and with hardly any water. However, they do like a sunny spot.

This shed is smothered in succulents – the perfect plants for a green roof, as they're extremely drought-tolerant.

Before you commit yourself

Not all structures are suitable for planting up. Ideally, the roof needs to have quite a shallow pitch to prevent the plants at the top being left with very little water, unless very drought-tolerant plants are used. In addition the roof itself must be sound and strong, since the plants and soil will be heavy, especially after rain. While it is reasonably straightforward to strengthen some structures, others will never be strong enough. Green roofs have become big business and a reputable company will be able to offer advice as well as installation.

Don't forget

You will need to carry out weeding and care for the plants, so don't plant a green roof if you have no head for heights.

Green roofs: what lies beneath

A living roof is built in layers. Systems vary, but these may include:

① A waterproof base layer, like a pond liner, essential to prevent plants damaging the roof of the building.

② A drainage layer of gravel or other coarse granular material, with plenty of air spaces.

③ A filter layer of semi-permeable landscape fabric to prevent soil particles from being washed away.

④ A top layer of low-fertility growing medium: a small proportion of soil or compost mixed with aggregate such as limestone chippings or crushed waste brick or concrete.

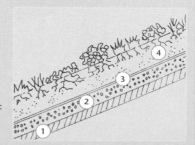

It is so important for children to get fresh air and exercise, and this is considerably more likely to happen if they have an outdoor space that they can call their own. With a little thought and design know-how, you can provide for their needs without compromising the appearance of your garden.

Designing with children in mind

Children grow up very quickly, so create play areas that you will be able to adapt as they get older. You probably want very young children to play close to the house and it is quite easy to tack a sandpit onto the patio or cover part of the surface with rubber matting for them to play on. When they grow older, the sandpit could become a small pond or flower bed and it is easy enough to replace matting with pavers.

Older children often prefer to be away from the adults, so you can put their play area in a less conspicuous place or hide it with plants or screening.

Play equipment

Ideally, choose wooden swings, climbing frames and playhouses in preference to plastic. These will blend in with your plants or they can be painted to suit their surroundings. Try to include a variety of things to stimulate your child's imagination. Hang colourful mobiles from trees and use containers and light-hearted ornaments to decorate their space.

This play area has plenty to keep a child happy, blends in with the surrounding plants and requires minimal maintenance, since the grass is artificial. Later, it will be easy to integrate into the garden.

Other simple but fun items are a walkway made from an old telegraph post (or something similar), with one side flattened, or stepping posts at different heights laid as a path. Both are easily integrated into any garden and could double as seating places.

There are plenty of ways to incorporate play areas into a small space.

① This sunken trampoline is also concealed by a slatted screen.

② A lidded sandpit sits happily at the edge of a decking patio.

Decorative garden structures

Garden structures can be purely for decoration or they can be functional as well as decorative. There is a huge choice available in a variety of materials, so you should find it easy to get something that answers your aesthetic needs as well as any practical requirements you might have. For plants to grow on these structures, *see* pages 92–6.

Pillars, colonnades and rustic tripods

Pillars, colonnades and tripods are frequently quite simple but can be highly decorative and usually have the additional role of being a support for climbing plants. They may be made of wood, metal, brick or stone.

Wood is versatile and you can find styles to fit into most garden situations. Rustic poles are excellent in cottage, seaside and country gardens, while planed wood is suitable for minimalist or formal spaces. Metal is more commonly found in modernist gardens and can be almost industrial or utilitarian in appearance. Stone and brick are often considered to be suitable for fairly traditional gardens, but they can also be used in a modern way.

Arbours

The primary role of an arbour is to provide a sheltered and private place to sit. It may also incorporate storage space under the seat and, of course, plants are easily grown over the top to create the effect of a bower. Arbours are most often made

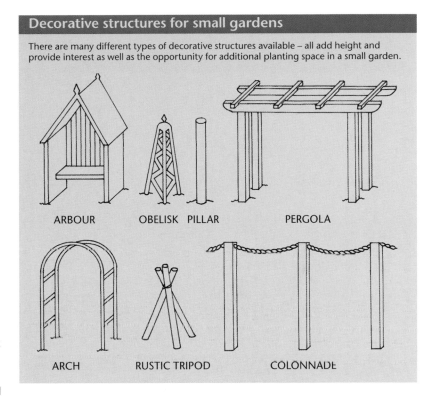

Decorative structures for small gardens

There are many different types of decorative structures available – all add height and provide interest as well as the opportunity for additional planting space in a small garden.

ARBOUR   OBELISK   PILLAR   PERGOLA

ARCH   RUSTIC TRIPOD   COLONNADE

of wood with a solid or trellis roof and sides. They usually have space for just one or two occupants, but can be larger – some are almost open-sided rooms, with seating for four or more. Their design varies from quite plain and rustic to elegant and complex.

Metal arbours, often referred to as 'gazebos', can be found second-hand as well as new. They can look quite delicate and very ornamental and the arch may be covered with curled and twisted wrought ironwork. They usually provide less privacy than wooden ones.

Lightweight, portable structures

Obelisks, wigwams and tripods are cheap, versatile ways to provide climbing frames for plants and decorate the garden. Woven hazel (far right) is rustic and looks particularly good in a country- or cottage-style garden, while a wooden obelisk (right) is suitable for a range of garden styles. If painted it can become quite an eye-catching feature.

Arches

Like pillars and colonnades, arches are both decorative features and climber supports. They are probably the most common of all garden structures, so there's a huge choice. The most usual materials are wood or metal, although you might prefer a custom-built arch of brick and stone.

Both wooden and metal arches can be plain or highly ornamental. The cheapest varieties tend to be basic and flimsy; if you pay more you'll get something that lasts longer and is much sturdier. However, sometimes lightweight may be just what you want. For example, willow arches or those made of woven hazel stems won't last forever but have a certain ethereal beauty.

Pergolas

A pergola is basically a series of linked arches that together make a structure that provides seclusion, some shelter and a frame for plants. Pergolas are most often rectangular, although they can also be square or a quarter-circle for a corner. They usually have pairs of uprights, but where space is limited the beams can be cantilevered from a house

The great thing about kit-form wooden garden structures is that they're fairly straightforward to build.

wall or you could position the beams along a single row of uprights.

Wood is the most common material, but metal, stone and brick can be used. It is also possible to mix materials and have, for example, wooden uprights and metal beams. Although pergolas are usually open, there is nothing to stop you having one with a roof or even one or more enclosed sides.

Many wooden pergolas come in kit form and are quite easy to erect. However, they must be firmly anchored in the ground to prevent movement or collapse during windy weather. If you're a DIY enthusiast, you could make one to your own specifications (*see* opposite).

For more on using pergolas in the garden *see* pages 22–3.

A simple wooden pergola provides the perfect frame for a climbing rose and creates a secluded spot for sitting out. This one has only four uprights, which gives more space for the chairs.

1

2

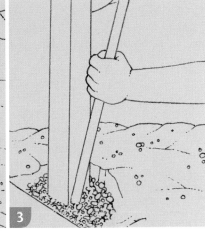

3

Mark the outline of the pergola, check the corners are square, then dig the post holes, 60cm (2ft) deep and about 30cm (1ft) across. If your ground tends to be wet, dig the post holes a little deeper and spread a layer of hardcore or scalpings in the bottom, compacting it well with a piece of timber. You may find it helpful to stand on a plank laid along the edge.

Set a post upright in the first hole and pack large stones around it to keep it in place. Check it is perpendicular. Ask a helper to hold the post in place while you fill the holes almost to the top with concrete (6:1 ballast : cement). Leave a gap of about 50mm (2in) at the top so you can cover the concrete with soil when the structure is complete.

Firm the concrete around each post with a piece of timber. Leave the concrete to harden and gain strength for a few days before fixing the roof structure. In the meantime, cut evenly spaced rectangular notches in the tops of the beams, into which the joists will eventually fit (*see* step 4). Position the notches for the end joists right next to the posts.

Don't forget

After you have cut pressure-treated timber, paint all the cut surfaces with timber preservative to prevent rot.

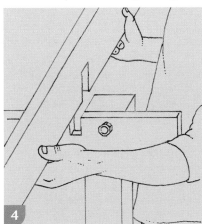

4

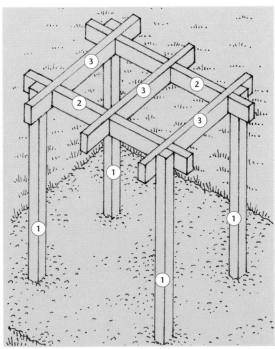

Use galvanized coach bolts to fix the beams lengthwise to the tops of the posts. Next, hold each joist in position so that there is an equal overhang on each side of the pergola and mark a notch in the bottom of the joist at each side, to correspond with the notches in the beams. Cut the notches, then fit the joists over the beams and secure them tightly from below with galvanized screws.

This view of the completed pergola shows how the posts ①, the two side beams ② and the joists ③ are joined together. Ideally, the posts will be 3m (10ft) or so long to allow for about 2.4m (8ft) above the ground and 60cm (2ft) below the ground to act as a firm anchor.

Pots and other containers

As well as giving you extra planting space, containers can provide some of the essentials of a good design, such as focal points and surprises, colour, texture and scale. Their design can set the entire style of a very small space, or create pockets of different themes in a larger garden. Like stage performers, pots of flowering plants can be moved into the limelight for their brief moment of glory, then slipped backstage once their flowers have faded.

Choosing pots

If you're starting from scratch, it makes good sense to plan your pot acquisitions to fit in with an overall scheme. Containers are available in a wide range of materials, from the traditional terracotta, stone or glazed clay to fibreglass or metal, and in every shape you can think of, from tall and square to shallow and round. The choice really depends on individual taste. Whatever you opt for, make sure that the pots are frost proof if you want them to stay outside all year round and that they have a reasonable drainage hole in the base to prevent waterlogging. Ideally, you need to raise the pot off the ground so it can drain more freely and earthworms and woodlice (which can be a nuisance in a pot) cannot get in.

Size matters

Unless you have something particular in mind, such as a display of alpines on shelves, avoid the very smallest pots. Plants in them soon run out of water and space, and the pots usually end up empty. If you plan to move pots in and out of view, choose medium-sized ones of about 30cm (12in) in diameter at the top. These are big enough to accommodate a wide range of plants, singly or in groups, and still be mobile. Watering once a day and feeding once a week should be

This rusted metal container is ideal for a young *Arbutus*. Its colour echoes that of the bark too.

adequate in summer. Pots much larger than this will be difficult to move, so give them permanent positions and plant them *in situ*.

Keep large pots for large or tall plants, for example shrubs and small trees or bamboos, tall lilies and climbers; smaller plants, even *en masse*, can look dwarfed by their size. In general, while a pot needs to be large enough not to stunt the root growth, it's best to choose something that makes the plant (or plants) look just slightly on the big side. One exception to this is trees and shrubs, which can be

Japanese blood-grass (*Imperata cylindrica* 'Rubra') looks good against terracotta.

The colours of this slate pot are a very close match for the plants inside.

Both colour and form are fitting in this blend of blue grass and silver pot.

Don't forget
If you're buying a special plant that is going to make a focal point, it might well be worth buying the container at the same time as the plant to ensure the two are perfectly matched.

top-heavy. In these cases, avoid pots that taper towards the base and make sure they are either weighted in the bottom or supported in some way so that they will not fall over. In general, avoid pots that narrow at the neck as it can be very hard to remove a plant for repotting without damaging it.

Design matters

Matching up the shape, form, texture and colour of plants and containers is by no means easy, so be prepared for a bit of trial and error before you get a combination that you feel happy with.

Getting the right look for your garden also depends on how you use the containers. For example, simple, strongly shaped pots all planted with the same species and arranged in a row would be ideal in a minimalist garden, where the emphasis is often on rhythm and repetition. In an informal or country garden, the same pots could be used but a more naturalistic, irregular grouping would probably be more appropriate.

Most gardeners amass a collection of pots over the years. This usually results in a mixed bag of styles and designs, but you can still produce an attractive and harmonious display. One of the easiest ways to do this is to make the plants create the harmony. This means using plants that are the same type or have similar flower or leaf colours or shapes (*see* right). Alternatively, if you are the sort of person who loves colour and cannot resist growing lots of different plants, make your schemes work by incorporating one

Pots made of GRP (Glass Reinforced Plastic) are an excellent choice for a roof terrace, balcony or window box; they are very lightweight and are available in metallic finishes and a wide range of colours.

A shallow-rooted succulent makes an ideal partner for this bowl-shaped concrete planter.

repeated theme. For example, fill several pots with the same type of plant then intersperse these evenly among the rest. They will create a visual flow through the display, tying it together and preventing a busy effect. You will get your wide range of plants, while still giving the impression of unity.

Several white agapanthus bring harmony to an assorted collection of containers.

Accommodating containers

When you start looking around your garden as a place to display pots and other containers, you will see possibilities everywhere.

At ground level

The most obvious place for containers is on the patio, deck or roof terrace. Arrange them informally in small groups or in a neat line or block. You can edge a seating area or path with a row of window boxes, for example. A matching set of pots of decreasing sizes will make a striking display, and you can link this visually with another group of similarly planted containers slightly offset or in another corner.

How to plant a basic container

Whatever type of container you're using, with the exception of open-sided hanging baskets (*see* opposite), the basic planting method and principles are the same.

■ Check the drainage hole in the bottom of the container is clear. Large pots need several holes. To deter vine weevils, lay a piece of fine mesh or old tights across the base of the pot before adding crocks (broken flowerpots) or bits of polystyrene to aid drainage.

■ Half fill the container with a layer of compost mixed with water-retaining granules and controlled-release fertilizer. Water the plants.

■ Remove one plant from its pot, gently loosen its roots and place it on the compost mix to check the depth. Allow about 1cm (½in) between the plant's 'neck' and the top of the container. Add or remove compost as necessary to get the level right.

■ Add the remaining plants and fill around the sides and in between the plants with more compost, firming as you go. Water well. With permanent plantings, add a layer of mulch (such as gravel) over the surface of the soil to retain moisture, suppress weeds and keep the roots cooler. Putting pot feet beneath the container will aid drainage, prevent waterlogging and deter earthworms and woodlice from getting in.

This range of plants and pots in many shapes and sizes is like a mixed flower border. The pots can be rearranged to highlight star performers.

In borders, plants can be given greater prominence by planting them in decorative tubs, raised above their bedfellows on upturned containers if need be. To ensure a succession of colour, slot pots of flowers into place wherever a section of border is looking dull. Plastic containers filled with spring bulbs or summer bedding can be put into the ground and then dug up to make room for the next lot of blooms.

Above ground level

A flight of steps is the ideal place for a display of containers. For a cascading effect, position the pots so that the plants on one step hide the pots on the step above. Or you could make the pots themselves part of a rhythmic display: matching pelargoniums in terracotta pots is a good example, but any lowish-growing plant works just as well. If you have steps up to your front door you could flank them with pairs of pots and plants. Clipped box (*Buxus*) or yew (*Taxus baccata*) are classic choices for a sophisticated look.

Windowsills are an obvious site for pots and window boxes (*see* page 111). If you have a balcony or roof terrace (*see* pages 114–15) you could attach window boxes to the railings.

Walls are the starting point for hanging baskets. Use them to frame the back door or to bring interest to a blank wall in a narrow side passage, basement area or courtyard, or even a garden shed. Choose plants to bring bursts of colour where needed or to fit in with the overall scheme of the garden.

Old tables, chairs, stools and step ladders are fun and versatile places for containers too. Stands are

Colourful food tins play an important part in this space-saving, stepped display of pink pelargoniums.

Succulents are happy in hanging baskets; they are drought-tolerant and have a long season of interest.

Don't forget

Weight is a major consideration on a roof terrace. Choose a lightweight pot and use polystyrene packing chips rather than gravel or crocks in the base.

available for large pots and hanging baskets, bringing the display nearer to eye level and allowing you to move them around as you wish.

Use brackets to attach shelves to the house wall or even to your fence or trellis. In the latter position, pots work best if they are hidden among the plants already clambering there, so their flowers seem to belong to them. Like containers 'planted' in borders, these displays can be changed with the seasons.

How to plant an open-sided hanging basket

The main difference between planting a basic container (*see* opposite) and an open-sided hanging basket is that you plant through the sides as well as the top, creating a full, all-round display of flowers and foliage. The method is a bit more fiddly, and you need a pre-formed liner (made of fibre, compressed paper pulp or sisal/jute mix), but the results certainly make the extra effort worthwhile. Place trailing plants around the sides and upright, bushy plants in the centre.

■ Place the hanging basket on an empty flowerpot to keep it steady. Put the liner inside and press it into place.

■ Using a sharp knife, make a cut in the sides of the liner for each plant. Add a layer of compost mixed with water-retaining granules and controlled-release fertilizer.

■ Plant through the holes. You can do this from the outside, pushing the rootball carefully through the gap, or from the inside, feeding the shoots through the hole. Build up another layer of compost around the sides and plant as you go.

■ Add more compost and water well (you'll need to water once a day in summer).

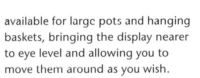

Shelves are a great way to display plants in their prime, such as these pansies in identical terracotta pots.

Once you have your garden laid out more or less as you would like it, with everything in place, you can focus on furnishing the patio and putting together the final details that will ensure your outdoor space can be used for much of the year. The concept of an outdoor room is not new, but the garden can only fulfil its role as an additional living space if you make it comfortable as well as enjoyable.

Furniture

Choose the best quality chairs and table that you can afford. These will last longer and be more pleasant to use than cheaper versions. Strong plastic furniture is fine and can be easier to move around, clean and store than wood, but wood often looks more the part. If possible, sit in the chairs before you buy them to make sure they are the right height and size. Nothing discourages sitting so much as a very small or hard seat.

If you've enough space, include a couple of loungers or choose convertible chairs. An excellent alternative is a hammock, which is easy to sling between pergola beams or a similarly sturdy structure. You've worked hard on your garden and you deserve to relax in it too.

Furnishings

You will want some cushions and other soft furnishings to make your seating area more attractive and homely. Cushions covered with removable washable fabrics are most versatile, but you can get a few seasons' wear from the wipe- or sponge-clean variety.

The best furniture is not only comfortable and attractive, it should also fit in with the setting.
① Brightly coloured waterproof fabric is an eye-catching feature of this wooden terrace. The bulky cushions look enticing.
② A hammock adds to the exotic flavour of this small deck and garden, while also making a pleasant place to spend a few hours relaxing.

Include a selection of colourful throws to alter the mood for different occasions and times of day.

If you often sit out in the evening, consider getting an awning or piece of sailcloth to erect over your pergola. This will make your seating space more private when you're using lights or

candles and will help to keep it warmer as the nights get chilly. A large umbrella can be put to similar use and will keep off light showers, too.

Lighting

Lighting is essential for evenings in the garden. The sort of dim light provided by candles is fine for eating, but if you want to read or write outdoors, electricity will allow for brighter lighting. It will also enable you to highlight plants or other features,

Don't forget

Carefully placed screens may help to muffle noise, so using them around a patio might be a good idea if you like late-night parties.

which will make the garden much more interesting at night. Get a professional electrician to install it. Not only will this ensure it is safe and legal, they will also be able to suggest ways to make the system versatile and extendable if you have any plans for future additions. (*See also* page 20.)

Heating and cooking

It's great to have heating in the garden for chilly nights, particularly as autumn approaches. Outdoor gas heaters are very effective and efficient; however, they are expensive and not at all environmentally friendly. Fire pits and chimineas are greener choices. Both are widely available in freestanding form, the main difference being a chiminea is usually more or less enclosed with a stout chimney, while a fire pit is more like an open fire; you could also dig a real pit for a fire, which is more authentic and very up to date. Both fire pits and chimineas can be used for cooking too.

If you barbecue a lot and have the space it's worth building a permanent barbecue that uses charcoal or bottled gas. Alternatively, there are any number of portable barbecues that meet most requirements. These range from the very cheap, disposable types, which are thrown away after one meal, to the pricier ones, some of which last years and cook food as well as – or better than – you could do indoors. For flavour, most people would say charcoal is best, but for even and

Don't forget

Be very careful with all forms of heating. They can get very hot and may damage plants, fabrics, UPVC and wooden window frames, and plastic downpipes.

Lighting need not be merely utilitarian, it can also be highly decorative.

① A strong beam picks out this bust on its simple plinth, creating dramatic areas of light and shade.

② Turquoise glass softens the lights that are set into the deck and lead to the table, creating a striking design feature.

③ Warm spotlights pick out the bamboo stems and make a perfect backdrop to this exotic-looking seating area.

thorough cooking, gas is more reliable and has the advantage of lighting first time and having several heat settings.

Decorative objects

Finally, have a little bit of fun personalizing your outdoor room. It's the tiny decorative details that give the garden its individual character and make it somewhere you love spending time. There are plenty of elements to choose from, including fairy lights, uplighters to accentuate particular plants or features, bubble fountains, sculptures and wall hangings.

A source of heat and light, a buried fire pit makes a strong statement on this patio.

Designing your small garden

When designing a garden, it's best to plan and execute the whole thing in one go. This means more upheaval and initial expense than if you were to do it piecemeal, but it will result in a more coherent end result. This chapter will lead you through the design process, from thinking about your space, wishes and needs to putting your plans into action. It concludes with five design case studies, which show how a plot only 8 x 10m (26 x 33ft) can be transformed in a number of different ways.

Assessing your garden

The first thing you need to do is to make a dispassionate assessment of the garden you have and decide what you want to keep and what you would like to change. Even a brand-new garden is rarely a completely blank canvas, and there are usually existing features and attributes that need to be considered before you create your design.

What is there already?

Imagine you're seeing your garden for the first time. Really look at it. Look at its position, its shape (see pages 28–9) and all the elements within it.

Get a large piece of paper and make a rough sketch of your house and garden as they are now. Include as much information as possible, such as where windows look onto the garden, the position of doors and other access points, as well as manhole covers and shed. Next, identify some of the fixed characteristics, for example the sunny, shady, windy or sheltered sites and any sloping areas (see page 60). Mark them on your sketch.

Jot down what you'd like to change and draw up a list of your priorities. In the end, you may well have to live with some features that you'd rather not, but it's good to consider each of them. It's well worth taking some photographs of the various elements that are already in place and the views from and to the house. These will come in useful when you're drawing up your plan (see page 64–6).

The view from inside

Make a point of looking at the garden from every window, including the upstairs windows. Remember that for a great many weeks of the year, the view of the garden is from the house, so this vista needs to be as interesting as possible. It should also be intriguing enough to tempt you out into the garden to experience it up-close. Again, make notes on what you see and think about what you'd like to do to improve the view.

Draw up a rough sketch of your garden and jot down a list of what you'd like to keep or lose.

Your garden should be interesting from inside too. Make sure it offers plenty to look at and tempt you out.

The boundaries and beyond

Once you've looked thoroughly at your garden, take a look at the property's perimeters. Consider the fencing, walling or hedging and decide whether it enhances the garden or makes it look smaller, more crowded or shabby.

Look beyond the boundaries, too. Is there anything there that you would rather not see and would like to hide? Or do you want to draw attention to a pleasant view? A favourite garden design trick is to blend the garden with what lies beyond to create a sense of greater space (see page 19).

Don't forget

Organize your notes into columns entitled 'Keep', 'Don't Keep' and 'Keep for now' – or something similar. This clarifies your priorities and helps you to assess the size of the job.

Don't forget

Getting to know your garden in detail before you start to spend any money will help you to avoid making costly mistakes and any of those 'if only ...' thoughts later on.

Considering the practicalities

You may have a clear vision of how your new garden should look, but you have to consider practical issues if the design is to be successful. To be able to position your seating in the best spot and grow healthy plants, you need to understand the garden's aspect and climate, the quality of the soil and its capacity for drainage, and the topography of the garden.

Aspect and microclimates

Most gardens have spots that are more sheltered, sunnier, more exposed, wetter or shadier than the garden as a whole. Get to know where these are, since they will have a bearing on where you should site key features such as the seating area, as well as the types of plants that feel at home there. Mark them on your sketch. Don't forget that the sun is lower in the sky in winter, so somewhere that is reasonably warm in summer might be in chilly shade later in the year.

Wind can be destructive, so it is useful to know how winds from different directions affect your garden. If you live in a built-up area, the wind may gust or eddy around buildings in surprising ways – for example, wind tunnels can form (*see* below left). But once you know this, you can allow for it in your design. A few carefully placed barriers, or two or three tough plants, might make the difference between a windswept, barren garden and one that is sheltered and cosy, even in the roughest of weather.

Soil and drainage

To stay healthy, most plants need soil of a reasonable quality and depth and fair drainage. However, there are plenty of plants that can survive in less-than-perfect conditions – stony, dry, damp and so on – so get to know your soil and you can choose the plants that are most likely to thrive in each spot.

Start by digging around in various parts of the garden to check the soil depth and find out what it's like. Is it fairly well drained, moist or wet? Buy a simple soil-testing kit from the garden centre and find out whether your soil is acid, alkaline or neutral. You can improve the drainage, moisture retention and nutrient levels in all soils by digging in plenty of humus-rich material, such as garden compost or well-rotted farmyard manure, but this takes time and effort so it's worth pinpointing the most needy areas and marking them on your sketch to make them a priority. Remember, the area beside fences and walls can be particularly dry because of the rain-shadow effect (*see* below left).

Topography

Slopes and undulations must be taken into account, since they will affect almost every other feature. A gentle slope near the proposed site of your patio means that soil will have to be moved or built up to create a level area, while sloping lawns and flower beds can be difficult to maintain, so terracing might be a better option.

Minor undulations in the garden are probably best evened out – note them on your sketch with arrows pointing up the slope. Where they are more pronounced, it could be easier to use them to your advantage. A reasonable-sized dip could become a pond or bog garden, for instance.

Narrow spaces between structures funnel the wind making it stronger and more damaging. Consider erecting or planting windbreaks.

Rain rarely falls vertically, so one side of a fence or wall is nearly always quite dry. Plant further out or water more often.

Identifying your needs

Once you've assessed the garden as it is, it's time to make a wish list of everything you'd like to include in your new garden. Try to prioritize and be realistic about what you need, can afford and have time for, and focus your mind on coming up with bright ideas for squeezing in something important. You may find the Garden-planning checklist (*see* page 63) helpful.

What's your garden for?

Start by thinking about what you're going to use your garden for. If you love entertaining or like to sit out and enjoy a bit of sunshine from time to time, top of your list should be a patio. Given the option, most people go for a level area at least big enough to fit a table and chairs comfortably (*see* page 67). However, if you don't have the space for this, low walls, steps and other 'incidental' hard landscaping can be used as seating without taking up too much room. When choosing a spot for the patio, think about what times of the day you're going to use it, whether it's going to be overlooked, whether you want mostly sun or sometimes shade. Don't automatically assume that just outside the kitchen door is the best place for it. If you can accommodate them, it's well worth fitting in two or even more seating areas for different times of day as the sun moves around the garden.

If you have children they will need the opportunity to let off steam, so the garden must be child-friendly as well as child-proof. If you have space, high on your list of priorities should be a swing, climbing frame or playhouse (*see* page 48).

Consider whether you just want ornamental plants, or whether you want to grow vegetables too. You don't need much space to grow a few crops and, in a very small garden, pots and raised beds can be used to plant crops intensively. Remember, the fence and house walls can also be clothed with plants.

Practical uses

Before you get too carried away with the fun side of the garden, take into account its practical purpose. The vast majority of gardens have at least one utilitarian function, even if it's only to provide somewhere to store the bikes or hang out the washing. Consider dustbins, compost, storage for garden furniture, toys and tools. Do you want a shed or a greenhouse? Both of these grow in importance the keener you become on gardening. An enthusiastic gardener will want somewhere – even just a shelf or workbench – to sow seeds and put them safely until they germinate, pot up plants and store potting compost. Fortunately, there's a wide range of smaller storage units to choose from and even washing lines have moved on – very few need to be left in full view when not in use, but you will need somewhere to put them out of the way.

> If you want to grow vegetables, allow space for a raised bed. Alternatively, you could put containers on your patio.

Wood predominates in this well-conceived tiny urban courtyard. The pergola complements the child's play area, while the climbers provide a subtle screen.

The financial side

Few of us have an unlimited budget, so as you start to build up a picture in your mind of what you would like, remember the cost. This might seem like dull advice, but it will prevent disappointment later on. Nowadays, it's very easy to check out a few prices on the internet to get a rough idea of whether what you have in mind is affordable. If it's not feasible now, you may be able to factor in improvements for the future, as and when money allows.

Time

Along with finance comes the other serious consideration: time. If you have plenty of time and are good at DIY, you'll be able to save money by doing some of the work yourself. You might choose to do the work over a few months or years, a little at a time. If a lot of excavation work is needed – for example, in order to level a sloping area for a patio – it makes good sense to use a contractor, since it will require a lot of hard labour and earth-moving equipment. This will allow you to enjoy your outdoor space that bit sooner than if you'd done it yourself.

Don't forget

By now your wish list may be very long and it might seem unlikely that you will be able to fit everything in. Look back at the notes you made when you assessed the space and see whether it's worth sacrificing something else.

Garden-planning checklist

The following questions will prompt you to consider your needs, taking your lifestyle, expectations and budget into account. They should help you to focus on priorities and to come up with a garden design that will suit you best.

Style and features

■ Are you interested in creating a particular 'style' of garden? If you prefer neatness or symmetry you might choose a minimalist or formal garden; if you like colour and have a relaxed approach consider a cottage garden, while a jungle garden might appeal if you want seclusion. (*See* pages 24–7.)

■ Have you taken into account the style and period of your home and surrounding buildings, and will your design and choice of materials seem appropriate in that setting?

■ Do you prefer hard surfaces such as paving, brick or decking, or loose surfaces such as gravel? (*See* pages 36–40.)

■ Is it important to you to source green products and use recycled materials? And do you prefer natural or man-made materials?

■ Have you thought about how changes of level, for instance terraces, steps and raised beds, might make your garden more interesting? (*See* pages 18–19 and 41–3.)

Plants and planting

■ How much time and inclination do you have to tend plants? Does the idea of plants that more or less look after themselves appeal, or do you enjoy nurturing them?

■ Have you thought about how you could use all the existing vertical surfaces in the garden for planting, for instance climbers against walls and fences? (*See* pages 92–6.)

■ Is there space to include a decorative feature to support plants, such as a pergola, arbour or obelisk? (*See* pages 49–51.)

■ Do fragrant plants appeal to you, and have you considered carefully where their scent may be best enjoyed? (*See* page 97.)

■ Do you plan to propagate plants and will you need to consider installing a greenhouse?

■ Do you want to grow vegetables and fruit, and if so would you like to allocate an area of the garden for the purpose or just have a few pots on the patio? (*See* pages 76–7 and 106–8.)

■ Is encouraging wildlife, for instance bees and butterflies, to your garden one of your priorities? (*See* page 98.)

■ Is there an eyesore you'd like to hide, and if so have you considered how you're going to achieve this with planting?

■ Have you thought about using plants underfoot instead of grass or to soften the edges of hard surfaces? (*See* page 36.)

■ Does the idea of a green roof appeal to you? (*See* page 47.)

■ Have you considered alternatives to solid paving in the front garden for car parking? For instance, have you looked at greener options, such as using gravel or a hybrid surface instead? (*See* pages 112–13.)

■ Are you making the most of containers in paved areas, and are you taking advantage of the fact that you can use pots to grow plants that won't grow in your soil?

Ages and needs

■ Do you have to consider a play area for children? Do you have trampolines, climbing frames and football pitches to take into consideration in your design? (*See* page 48.)

■ Should you be thinking about designing the garden with the increasing ages of the garden's users in mind? Can children's play areas adapt as they grow older? Will you be able to keep up with the demands of the garden as you become less energetic?

■ If you have children or grandchildren, have you considered the dangers of a pond, the fact that decking is more child-friendly than paving, and that some plants are toxic or cause skin irritations?

■ Do you have pets to consider? If so, are the boundaries sufficiently secure for the animals to run free? Do you need to allow space for equipment, such as a hutch or a run?

Dining and relaxing

■ Do you like to eat and entertain outdoors? If so, how many people do you need to accommodate on the patio on a regular basis? (*See* page 67.)

■ Would you like to include a cooking area in the garden, such as a barbecue (built-in or portable) or fire pit? (*See* pages 57 and 74–5.)

■ Does the idea of a built-in bar or fridge appeal? (*See* pages 68–9.)

■ Have you thought about the best position, or positions, for secluded seating areas where you can sit and admire your plants?

■ If privacy is important to you, have you considered how you can screen out unwanted exposure?

■ Do you find the idea of water relaxing, and if so do you prefer the trickling sound of running water or the calm of still water? (*See* pages 44–5.)

Storage and utilities

■ Think about all the items you need to store. Might there be options other than, or in addition to, the usual garden shed, for instance bikes hanging on walls or tools in storage boxes.

■ Have you thought about doubling up seating areas and storage if space is at a premium? (*See* page 46.)

■ Would you like to screen off your garden shed, or would you prefer to make a decorative feature of it? (*See* page 46.)

■ Have you thought about different shapes and styles of garden sheds other than the usual apex-roof variety?

■ Do you need to allow for space for recycling storage and refuse bins? If so, have you considered where best to position them so that they are out of the way? (*See* page 46.)

■ How many compost bins do you have space for (three is ideal, but few small gardens will have the space)? Would a wormery be a good alternative?

■ Have you considered whether a rotary clothes dryer or a retractable washing line would best suit your needs and space?

Budget and skills

■ Is the garden a long-term investment that you're going to enjoy for decades, or might you be moving on within a few years?

■ Are you designing the garden purely for yourself and your family, or should you consider the needs of a future buyer?

■ Are your plans realistic, and can you afford to carry them out in their entirety, or might it be worth economizing in some areas, for instance the cost of materials?

■ Are you able to create the design yourself or will you need the help of a professional garden designer?

■ Will you need to hire labour to carry out your design plans, or are you someone who enjoys doing the work yourself?

From dreams to reality

You've assessed your garden in its current state and have made a wish list of what you'd like to include in your new design. Perhaps you also have an idea of what garden style you would like. Now is the time to draw up a good scale plan of the garden, start adding the new elements and see if your ideas can be put into practice in the space given. A scale drawing prevents all kinds of mistakes, such as a patio that's too small, a shed that's too large, or flower beds that are too narrow.

Drawing up a scale plan

The first step is to measure your garden accurately using a long tape measure. Choose a fixed line, such as the house wall, to use as your baseline and measure out from this using the tape measure. Measure the distances to all the boundary lines,

Make sure you know the precise positions of all the unmovable features in your garden and write them down.

the length of the perimeters and the positions of any features that you want to keep or must retain, such as paths, sheds and manhole covers.

Transfer the measurements onto a scale diagram. Use graph paper or paper marked with squares and choose a simple scale. For a small garden, a scale of 1:50 makes good sense (that is, 1cm on the plan = 50cm on the site).

Starting with scribbles

Once you have a reasonable scale plan showing your garden and its various existing components, make photocopies of the plan and use these to develop your final design.

Look back at pages 28–9 and at the design Case Studies on pages 68–77 for ideas on using various simple patterns to make the most of your garden's particular shape and size and to create different effects. You might like to take one of your copies and, with a soft pencil and eraser, quickly play around with, say, interlocking squares and rectangles of various sizes and at different angles until you come up with a

couple of basic design patterns that appeal. Remember, keep it simple.

Next, either on tracing paper laid over the design patterns, or on a copy of your scale plan, roughly indicate positions for your wish-list elements: use squiggles for a good view or an eyesore, crosshatching for shady spots near fences or buildings, circles for your seating area, shed and washing line. Make sketchy lines for flower beds. Often in a small garden there are only two or three sensible positions for the main structures and just a few options for hard landscaping. These will become clearer as you start to add each item.

You can keep making adjustments until the rough positions of the wish-list elements fit in with your design patterns. You are still working with very rough scribbles – nothing precise, and it will take a number of goes before it looks like it might work – a bit like doing a jigsaw.

Making a detailed plan

Now start drawing up a more detailed plan. You can use graph or squared paper again, or you might like to transfer the measurements to a plain sheet of paper. It is a matter of what you find easier. Pre-drawn lines can be a help for marking out structures that have straight edges,

Computer-aided design

You might prefer to key your measurements (and sometimes upload photographs) into one of the computer-aided design (CAD) programs that are available on CD-ROM, DVD or online. The software will then create a 3-D template of your garden. Using this, you can experiment with different design options and materials until you have a scheme you are happy with.

such as the patio and shed, but they can sometimes be a hindrance, or an unwanted influence on freer shapes.

You might find it helpful to make cut-out shapes to scale of some features, such as patios, benches and sheds, so you can play around with their positions on the plan.

Where to begin

Every garden is unique, so it's impossible to be exact about how it should be put together, but it's often best to begin by marking up the key features using your sketches to help with positioning.

A good starting point is likely to be the patio and paths. These will be the most used parts of the garden, so it's vital that you get them in the right place. They will also help to dictate the positions of other features. For example, if there is only one obvious place for the path, you may find you will need to put in a short flight of steps, or this may indicate the perfect place for the washing line or shed, both of which should be reached by a path.

Spatial relationships

By working on the layout of the hard landscaping, you will start to exercise your inventive muscles and begin to see the possibilities of your site. Even just thinking clearly about shapes and sizes will bring other ideas to mind and you should find your plans really begin to take

shape. For example, you might want a small tree beside the patio. Mark this in. From here you might see a spot for another tree to act as a complement to the first. With these two in place, you ought to think about the triangle effect (*see* page 15) and consider adding some lower plants. Don't worry about particular plants yet, just get the general shape of the flower beds down. One of the benefits of drawing a plan on paper is that you can see opportunities for balancing elements, making subtle patterns and echoing features, all of which help to get a better final result. And the great thing is you still have time to change your mind.

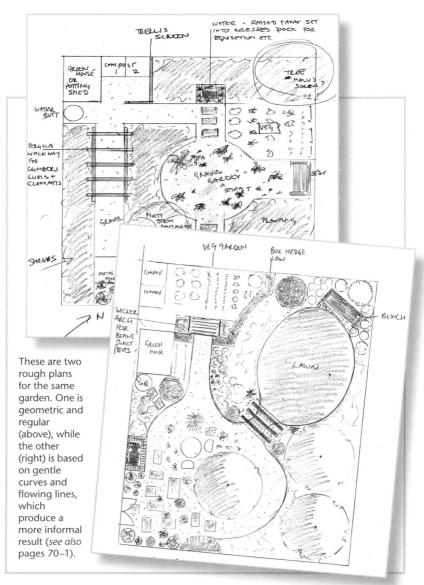

These are two rough plans for the same garden. One is geometric and regular (above), while the other (right) is based on gentle curves and flowing lines, which produce a more informal result (*see also* pages 70–1).

> ### Don't forget
>
> Discover where your electricity cables, phone lines and water pipes are buried. You really do not want to find these by mistake! You may need to contact the relevant utility companies.

Making planting plans

One of the best ways to decide what to plant and where is to draw each of your flower beds, to scale, and mark the plants on them – use circles. If you already know what plants you are going to use, check how wide they will grow, so you can leave them a reasonable amount of room to grow into. Alternatively, make brief notes and add names later. For example, 'medium-sized, pink, autumn-flowering perennial' could become *Aster ericoides* 'Pink Cloud'. The next few pages contain some ideas for garden layouts along with ideas for planting to help you on your way.

Turning plans into reality

You're now ready to transfer your design from a plan to the ground. At this point you can get the help of a builder or garden landscaper, or you can get out into the garden and begin marking up what goes where yourself. First, you'll need to measure the new elements on your plan and multiply them to full scale. Make a note of the real sizes on the drawing.

Drive pegs into the ground at several points along the outline of the proposed patio or path, for instance, then link the shapes with rope or string, or with a hosepipe fixed to the ground with wire hoops. Use long canes to mark the position of trees and other tall features to get an idea of how the layout will look. Look at your handiwork from various places in the garden and house – go upstairs and look out of a window. You still have time to make adjustments. When you're finally happy, mark out the design more permanently with landscaper's spray paint or a trail of dry sand.

Trying out the options

Although drawing shapes on paper is helpful in creating your basic garden design, there comes a time when you need to get out there and see what they look like for real. A length of hosepipe will allow you to try out the effect of various curves in the garden and you can make small adjustments by eye.

For straight lines, use string and pegs or bamboo canes. Stand back to check you're happy with what you've done before finalizing the position of flower beds, paths, seating areas and so on (*see* left). Even then, it's perfectly possible that you'll want to make further changes before digging starts.

Use pegs and string to mark out the proposed outline of lawns, flower beds, seating areas and paths.

When you're happy with the outlines, use sand or landscaper's spray paint to indicate the exact shapes.

Don't forget

The clearer and more detailed your plan, the easier it will be to transfer it to the garden. Be prepared to be flexible – even with the best-laid plans, last-minute adaptations are sometimes necessary.

Recommended measurements

It's a common mistake, especially when designing a small garden, to allow insufficient space for the various garden elements and features. It's very easy to make patios too small or borders and paths too narrow. Make sure your pergola or arch will be tall and wide enough to walk through comfortably. Sizes that look fine on paper can be too large or small in reality, particularly once the plants have grown. Below are some measurements to consider at the planning stage.

GARDEN FEATURE	DESIGN/PRACTICAL CONSIDERATIONS	RECOMMENDED MEASUREMENTS
Borders	Very narrow borders can look mean and won't accommodate a lot of plants; narrow borders can make a narrow garden look narrower.	Minimum width: 1.2–1.5m (4–5ft)
Raised beds	Beds need to be sufficiently deep and wide to accommodate plants' roots and so the plants don't dry out too quickly, but not so wide that they are difficult to maintain.	Maximum width: Bed you can access from one side only 75cm (2½ft); bed you can access from both sides 1.5m (5ft) Minimum depth: 45cm (18in); ideally 60cm (2ft)
Climbers and wall plants	Sufficient distance from the wall is vital to allow space for the plant's roots to spread; also, the base of the wall tends to be dry because of the rain-shadow effect (*see* page 60), the wall's foundations, and occasionally rubble.	Minimum distance from wall: 30–45cm (12–18in). You may be able to plant closer to a fence, depending on soil conditions.
Lawn	Manoeuvring a lawnmower in a small space is awkward and limits the surrounding planting; also, a really tiny lawn can look rather silly!	Minimum size: 3 x 3m (10 x 10ft); anything smaller and it is better to consider alternatives (*see* pages 36–40)
Patio/dining area	The area must be sufficiently large to accommodate a table and chairs, with space to have the chairs pushed back and for people to walk around as well as sit down.	For two people sitting at a table (and chairs): paved area minimum 2.5 x 1.5m (8 x 5ft) For six people (round table): paved area minimum 3.5 x 3.5m (12 x 12ft) For eight people (rectangular table): paved area minimum 4.5 x 3.5m (15 x 12ft)
Paths	Although a narrow path can be effective in infrequently used parts of the garden, main paths need to be wide enough to accommodate people, wheelbarrows and so on without the user feeling cramped, particularly when plants spill over the edges.	For one person walking: 60cm (2ft) For two people walking: 1.2m (4ft) For a wheelchair: 1.2m (4ft) to allow for comfortable turnaround For a wheelbarrow: minimum width 60cm (2ft)
Steps	It's a mistake to use indoor step measurements for outdoor steps. Outdoors, these will seem too steep and narrow, and they're more difficult to negotiate in wet or icy weather. Make the treads deeper, the risers lower and the width as wide as practicable.	Treads: Minimum 30cm (12in) from front to back Risers: Ideally 10–15cm (4–6in); 17cm (7in) is acceptable Width: Minimum 60cm (2ft)
Pergolas	Pergolas are often sold in kit form of a set height and width. Choose one that allows for plant growth up the pillars and over the top while still giving you room to pass through comfortably.	Height: Minimum 2.3m (7½ft) above ground; posts must be 60cm (2ft) longer if fixing in concrete Width: Minimum 1.2–2m (4–6ft)

Designed for people who have little time to garden, this is a comfortable and stylish outdoor room for eating, entertaining and relaxing. The minimalist, open-plan living area of the house has fully glazed, bi-fold doors that open onto the terrace. Careful use of lighting and informal seating complement the interior. Interlocking squares and rectangles create the main shapes in this design, while the asymmetry gives it a formal style with a modern look. The low-maintenance garden has three main areas: a deck; a reflective water pool; and a sunken 'chill-out' area.

The deck

Smooth decking boards, stained to match the interior timber flooring and laid at right angles to the house, lead the eye out into the garden.

Cooking and dining

A metal table and matching chairs help to give a contemporary feel to the deck. A stainless-steel gas barbecue on wheels is stored neatly away, but is quickly accessible to provide a practical outdoor dining space.

Planters

Clipped box (*Buxus*) balls in square GRP (Glass Reinforced Plastic) planters with a metallic, textured finish complement the furniture and offer lightweight planting space on either side of the barbecue. On the opposite boundary, a long trough in the same material is planted with the fragrant, white-flowered evergreen star jasmine (*Trachelospermum jasminoides*) underplanted with herbs, to provide low-maintenance, year-round structural planting and screening.

The reflective water pool

A sunken pool divides the deck and 'chill-out' area. Edged with a line of paving, the pool makes a feature of the weather with the play of light, sky, clouds and rain. At each end a square

bed is planted with a clipped box cube. A deck path over the pool leads to steps down to the 'chill-out' area.

The sunken 'chill-out' area

Surrounding retaining walls provide an intimate feel to a space for sofa-type cane seating. Buff stone paving matches the pool edging, linking the areas of the garden. A timber-clad unit to house an outdoor fridge and bar or storage doubles as a bench.

Planting

The simple planting scheme requires little maintenance. Five white-stemmed silver birches (*Betula utilis* var. *jacquemontii*) provide the key structural planting. Each tree is surrounded by a cube of clipped box (*Buxus*) that hides a small uplighter to illuminate the white stems at night. Between the trees, a variegated evergreen hedge of *Pittosporum tenuifolium* 'Silver Queen' creates a feeling of enclosure. Three sunken beds are planted with *Astelia chathamica* 'Silver Spear' and ground cover; the largest contains grasses too.

Trellis screening

A timber lateral trellis screen around the entire garden leads the eye out into the garden and creates a feeling of privacy and intimacy. Gaps between the battens allow light to pass through.

THE KEY ELEMENTS

Size of garden: 8 x 10m (26 x 33ft)

THE DECK

1 LONG TROUGH
Planted with an evergreen climber

2 DINING AREA
Table and seating for four

3 DECKING
Extends the house into the garden

4 BARBECUE
With space around it for entertaining

5 SQUARE PLANTERS x 2
Containing box balls, positioned on either side of the barbecue

THE REFLECTIVE WATER POOL

6 SQUARE BEDS x 2
With box cubes, at each end of the pool

7 PAVED EDGING TO THE POOL
Matches stone used in 'chill-out' area

8 DECK PATH
Forms a bridge over the water

9 STEPS
Lead down to informal sitting area

THE 'CHILL-OUT' AREA

10 PAVING
Light-coloured buff stone

11 FURNITURE
Designed for outdoor use

12 BUILT-IN STORAGE
Doubles as bench for seating

13 SUNKEN PLANTING BEDS x 3
With evergreen plants and ground cover

14 LOW RETAINING WALL
At sitting height for extra guests

15 RAISED BEDS WITH LIGHTING
On three sides, with trees and hedging

16 LATERAL TRELLIS SCREENING
All the way round the perimeter

Don't forget

A pool requires careful design and construction and some maintenance. An alternative could be a bed planted with see-through grasses.

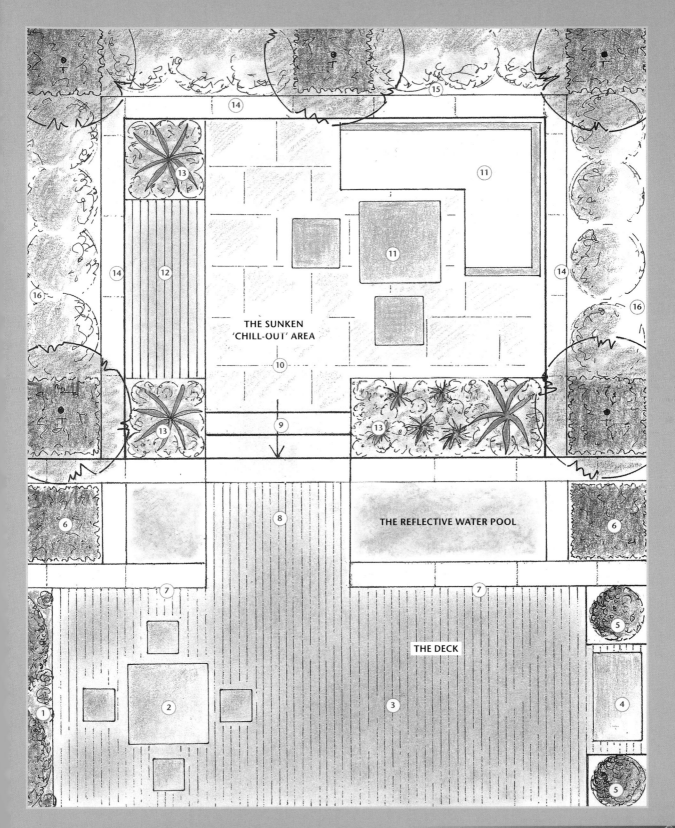

THE SUNKEN 'CHILL-OUT' AREA

THE REFLECTIVE WATER POOL

THE DECK

Plantaholic's garden

This is a garden for a plant-lover, combining traditional cottage-garden elements with practical space for cultivation. The design uses circles, curves and an ellipse to create flowing, informal spaces that allow the garden to be revealed in stages. There are four main areas: a gravel garden with seating and a small water feature; a 'productive' garden featuring a greenhouse, compost area and vegetable plot; a lawn surrounded by sunny borders with a bench seat; and a spring garden.

The gravel garden

French windows open onto an area with paving slabs randomly set in gravel. Plants spill over the gravel and are allowed to self-seed, creating a soft, *ad hoc* feel. A bistro-style table and chairs are tucked between plants that thrive in the dry conditions of gravel, such as *Eryngium giganteum* 'Silver Ghost', *Gaura lindheimeri*, *Stipa gigantea*, *Stipa tenuissima*, *Verbena bonariensis* and hollyhocks (*Alcea*).

Pots and containers

A changing array of terracotta pots and planters of varying shapes and sizes are planted with herbs, seasonal bulbs and annuals. Randomly placed around the door, they provide year-round colour.

Water feature

A raised brick pool collects water from a reconstituted-stone 'Green Man' water spout set into a wall and makes a focal point for the seating area. The sound of water can muffle traffic noise.

The productive garden

A stepping-stone path leads off the gravel garden, through planting, to the water butt, which collects water from the roof of a small greenhouse set back from a gravel path. The main, straight gravel path then continues under a willow arch, which supports climbing beans and peas, to reach a vegetable bed and a compost area. This corner of the garden is edged with a decorative, low box (*Buxus*) hedge.

The lawn and sunny borders

A timber pergola forms an entrance from the gravel garden to the area of lawn and sunny borders, and provides the support for repeat-flowering roses and clematis. The ellipse-shaped lawn and sweeping curved borders that surround it create the feeling of a garden within a garden. Densely planted, the borders are a mixture of colourful and scented plants typical of the cottage-garden style, such as *Alchemilla mollis*, delphiniums, pinks (*Dianthus*), *Phlox paniculata* and shrub roses. A bench set into the planting provides a 'destination' for the journey through the garden, and a secluded place to take a break from work.

The spring garden

From the lawn area, the gravel path curves back towards the house, through the spring garden and between three trees: *Prunus* 'Pandora', *Malus* 'John Downie' and *Sorbus vilmorinii*, which all have more than one season of interest. This shadier part of the garden is planted with perennials and bulbs that are in their prime in spring, such as columbine (*Aquilegia*), hellebores (*Helleborus*), daffodils (*Narcissus*), primulas and pulmonaria.

THE KEY ELEMENTS

Size of garden: 8 x 10m (26 x 33ft)

THE GRAVEL GARDEN

1 CONTAINERS
For year-round seasonal colour

2 STEPPING STONES
Set in gravel, lead to table and chairs

3 PLANTS IN THE GROUND
Drought-tolerant plants set in gravel

4 WATER FEATURE
Focal point for the seating area

5 SEATING AREA
Small table and chairs for two

THE PRODUCTIVE GARDEN

6 WATER BUTT
Essential for collecting rainwater

7 GREENHOUSE
Compact, aluminium alloy and glass

8 STRAIGHT PATH
Gravel, leading to the vegetable plot

9 WILLOW ARCH
Provides vertical growing space

10 COMPOSTING AREA
Space for at least two compost bins

11 VEGETABLE PLOT
For a year-round supply of vegetables

12 LOW BOX HEDGE
Defines the vegetable plot

THE LAWN AND SUNNY BORDERS

13 BENCH
For contemplation

14 PERGOLA
Divider and support for climbers

THE SPRING GARDEN

15 CURVED PATH
Through the spring garden

16 TREES x 3
Chosen for added value and underplanted with bulbs and perennials

Don't forget

Create areas that peak at different times of the year; by shifting the focus from season to season, you effectively have several gardens.

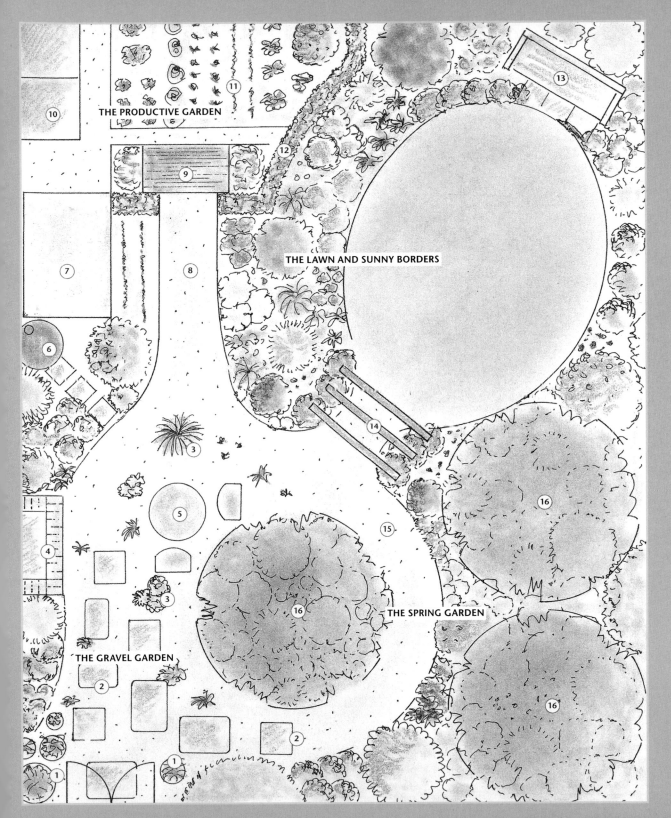

THE PRODUCTIVE GARDEN

THE LAWN AND SUNNY BORDERS

THE SPRING GARDEN

THE GRAVEL GARDEN

Designed for everyday use by all family members, this garden is a practical outside space for eating, relaxing, playing and learning, and can easily be adapted as the children grow up. The diagonal design helps move the eye across the garden at its longest point and gives a feeling of movement and energy. It also enables the space to be divided into 'rooms' with different uses. There are four main areas: a terrace; a lawn; a play area; and a utility area.

The terrace

Stone paving directly outside the house makes a practical area for outdoor family dining. The paving is laid diagonally to tie into the overall theme. There is space for a movable barbecue against the boundary fence. Children may like to grow seasonal plants in the brightly coloured planters.

The lawn

The lawn (maximum length and width 5.8 x 3.5m/19 x 12ft) is set on the diagonal and provides a soft surface for children.

A timber bench is built into the corner of the lawn, backed with a trellis screen. Occasional cushions make this a pleasant spot for reading or for adults to sit while children play close by.

The play area

A swing and a freestanding wooden sandpit with a lid (*see* page 48) could be replaced with a trampoline or table-tennis table. Suitable surface options include play bark, rubber mats, rubber chippings and artificial grass. A willow wigwam amid planting in the far corner makes a fun 'secret' den.

A small raised, timber-edged bed is ideal for children to learn about plants and start growing their own. Squash, beans of different colours and sweetcorn are easy to grow, as are blueberries and flowers such as sunflowers and sweet peas.

The utility area

A timber trellis screen and gate keep young children out of the area. A shed with a sedum roof (*see* page 47) stores bikes and garden tools, and a small unit houses recycling boxes. A wormery quickly turns kitchen waste into compost for use on the garden. There is also a water butt, a rotary clothes dryer and a small herb bed. A gravel surface is a practical option here.

The planting

A modern planting palette uses a mix of well-behaved, low-maintenance shrubs, grasses and perennials to balance shape, height, structure, texture and colour with seasonal interest. These could include:

Shrubs – *Choisya* × *dewitteana* 'Aztec Pearl', *Lavandula angustifolia* 'Hidcote', *Photinia* × *fraseri* 'Red Robin', *Sarcococca confusa*

Grasses – *Anemanthele lessoniana*, *Calamagrostis* × *acutiflora* 'Overdam', *Carex testacea*, *Festuca glauca* 'Elijah Blue', *Imperata cylindrica* 'Rubra'

Perennials – *Anemone* × *hybrida* 'Honorine Jobert', *Geranium* 'Rozanne', *Hemerocallis* 'Golden Chimes', *Libertia grandiflora*, *Penstemon* 'Garnet'.

Wildlife

A bird table in a border can be seen from the house and seating areas. A bird bath, bug hotel and nesting boxes also encourage wildlife (*see also* page 98).

THE KEY ELEMENTS

Size of garden: 8 x 10m (26 x 33ft)

THE TERRACE

1 PAVING
Indian sandstone laid in regular pattern

2 PLANTERS
Brightly coloured, for added interest

3 BARBECUE
On wheels, readily accessible

4 SEATING
Table and chairs for five

THE LAWN

5 BIRD TABLE
In planting, to give birds cover

6 CORNER BENCH
Near play area; good focal point

THE PLAY AREA

7 FLEXIBLE PLAY SPACE
Adapt as children's interests change

8 WILLOW WIGWAM
Den hidden in planting

9 CHILDREN'S VEGETABLE AND FLOWER GARDEN
Timber-edged raised bed

THE UTILITY AREA

10 TRELLIS SCREEN WITH GATE
Separates and screens the area

11 ROTARY CLOTHES DRYER
Screened by trellis

12 WATER BUTT
Collects water from shed roof

13 SHED
With sedum roof; for bikes, tools, etc

14 STORAGE FOR RECYCLING BOXES
Encourages care for the environment and frees up space in the house

15 WORMERY
Space-saving compost-maker

Don't forget

It's a good idea if you're planting a lawn with children in mind to use a hardwearing grass-seed mixture, which will withstand the wear and tear of family life. It is also more tolerant of neglect than luxury grass-seed mixtures.

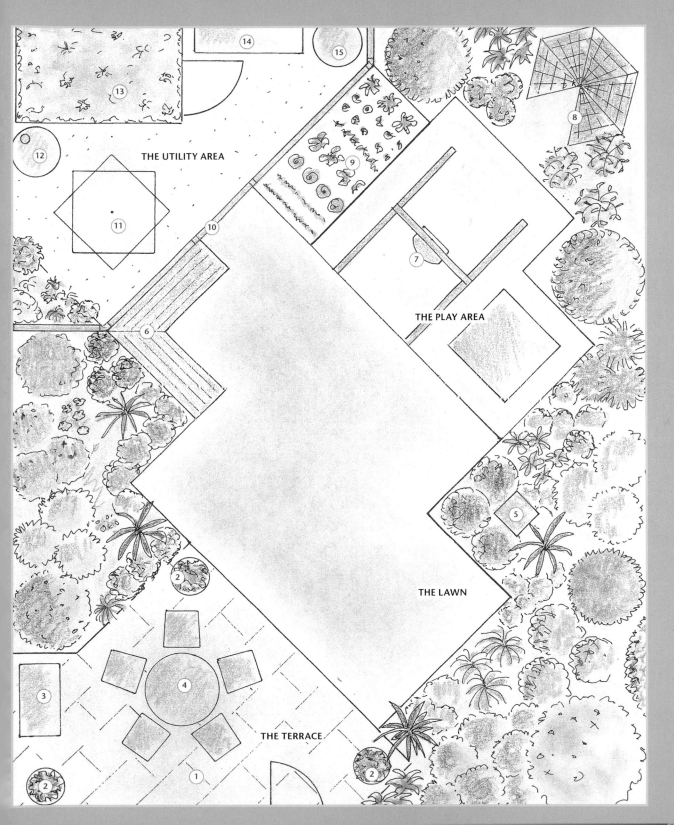

THE UTILITY AREA

THE PLAY AREA

THE LAWN

THE TERRACE

This is a fun, funky garden using large-leaved and exotic-looking plants with bright colours to evoke a tropical paradise. It is ideal for DIY enthusiasts, with home-made elements allowing for use of recycled materials and found objects. The design uses rectangles, curves and circles, or part-circles, to create an informal, flowing space with an unstructured feel. There are four key areas: a dining deck; a boardwalk; a secluded lounging deck with a fire pit; and a stepping-stone path leading to a hammock and a rustic hut.

The dining deck

The timber deck area immediately outside the house provides access to the garden and creates an area for outdoor dining. Large tree stumps act as stools, and a rustic table is made from recycled timber offcuts.

Planters

Rusted-metal containers for structural plants, such as a small Canary Island date palm (*Phoenix canariensis*) or yucca lookalike *Beschorneria yuccoides*, with its red flower spikes, contribute to the jungle theme.

The boardwalk

A curved path, built from timber offcuts, large deck boards or old scaffold boards, cut to various shapes and sizes, creates a haphazard feel. It is flanked by colourful, tropical-looking plants, including cannas, crocosmias, dahlias and daylilies (*Hemerocallis*). Using plants of different heights enhances the sense of exploration. Bamboo posts of varying sizes are set among the plants to add height and lead the eye to what lies ahead.

The secluded lounging deck

A circular deck surrounded by tall, large-leaved plants, such as bamboo, palms and a banana tree, makes a secluded area for relaxation. A hole cut into the decking allows for a tall

Cordyline to be planted so that it looks as if the deck were built around it. Big outdoor beanbags and a metal Indian cooking pot used as a fire pit make this a fun place to sit in the evening.

The stepping-stone path

A stepping-stone path made of circular pieces of timber or sawn-off ends of tree trunk, set informally into planting under the banana tree, leads first to a hammock suspended from rustic timber posts and beyond to a hut.

The rustic hut

For storage of tools, the self-built hut is made from round, upright timber posts, with a final covering of turf on the roof.

The planting

Exotic-looking plants are used to create the jungle feel in this garden. The perimeter is planted with bamboos (*Phyllostachys nigra* and *Phyllostachys aurea*) for screening. Large, strategically placed palms, such as *Trachycarpus fortunei* or *Phoenix canariensis*, create a tropical ambience. Ferns such as *Dryopteris* and *Polystichum* will look good at a lower level, while in a shady corner by the dining deck, a canopy of tree ferns (*Dicksonia antarctica*) of different heights creates a sculptural feature. Most of these plants are hardy in Britain but some may need protection in winter. (*See also* page 109.)

THE KEY ELEMENTS

Size of garden: 8 x 10m (26 x 33ft)

THE DINING DECK

1 DECKING
Constructed of wide deck boards or recycled scaffold boards

2 PLANTERS
Rusted metal containers, for tall structural plants

3 FURNITURE
Made from tree stumps and recycled timber offcuts

4 GLADE OF TREE FERNS
A jungle-like canopy planted near the dining deck

THE BOARDWALK

5 EXOTIC GROVE
Colourful planting either side of a path of randomly sized boards

6 BAMBOO POSTS
Of varying sizes, set into the planting beside the boardwalk

THE SECLUDED LOUNGING DECK

7 THE FIRE PIT
Freestanding or set into the ground; provides heat and light after dark

8 BEANBAGS
Of colourful, showerproof material

9 PLANTING
Large, leafy plants, including a banana tree, surrounding the deck

THE STEPPING-STONE PATH

10 HAMMOCK
For relaxation within the 'jungle'

11 STORAGE HUT
Self-built; or a standard shed embellished with rush matting

12 BAMBOO SCREENING
Encloses the whole garden

Don't forget

Extensive use of tall plants heightens the sense of drama, as do big leaves and lush foliage. Paradoxically perhaps, large plants can create the impression that a small garden is bigger than it actually is.

THE SECLUDED
LOUNGING DECK

THE STEPPING-STONE
PATH

THE BOARDWALK

THE DINING DECK

| Kitchen garden

Keen cooks appreciate having the freshest ingredients at their fingertips and a dedicated kitchen garden is often just what they need. This design takes its inspiration from the traditional French potager with fruit, vegetables, herbs and a cutting garden. The symmetrical cross-shape of the design immediately creates a formal and traditional feel. The eye is drawn to the centre, where a strong focal point anchors the design. The garden is divided into two main areas: the raised terrace and the potager.

The raised terrace

A wide, paved terrace adjoins the house, providing space for a long, wooden table and chairs for outdoor dining. There are flower beds on either side: to the right, box (*Buxus*) balls are interspersed with blue-flowered *Geranium* 'Rozanne', and to the left a pink climbing rose (*Rosa* 'Constance Spry') is planted against the wall.

Against the house wall, three reconstituted-stone planters with box balls echo traditional formal gardens.

Walls and steps

A low brick wall edges the terrace, and brick steps lead down to the kitchen garden. To the left side of the steps is a lavender hedge – a traditional culinary plant, it offers fragrance and attracts pollinating insects.

The potager

Brick paths dissect the kitchen garden, providing the main route across the space and additional, narrower access paths. These paths create a geometric pattern on the ground plan. (*See* page 39 for a selection of different brick and paving patterns.)

Obelisks

Timber obelisks, painted grey-green, provide support for vegetables as well as adding useful year-round height and structure in the garden (*see* page 49).

The central parterre

Four box balls link low box hedges to form the parterre, or ornamental flower bed. A standard bay (*Laurus nobilis*) provides height in the middle. It is underplanted with catmint (*Nepeta* × *faassenii*), an aromatic loved by bees.

Fruit and vegetables

Four square planting beds allow for vegetable crop rotation. Fruit bushes are located against the rear and side walls. Stepover fruit trees (*see* page 108) line the central brick paths, and espalier fruit trees and bushes are grown against the left wall, including currants and two gooseberry bushes.

Arbour

Made from timber and clad with fragrant roses, this houses a seat – a place to rest and enjoy the garden. Beds to either side are planted with herbs and flowers for the house.

Tool store and compost area

There is a timber store for tools against the right-hand wall. This space could be divided to fit in a small cold frame. There is a compost bin on either side of the tool store.

Sculpture

A sculpture is positioned at the end of the central access path to provide a focal point from the terrace.

THE KEY ELEMENTS

Size of garden: 8 x 10m (26 x 33ft)

THE RAISED TERRACE

1 PAVING
Indian sandstone (mixed sizes) laid in a random pattern

2 PLANTERS
Traditional-style container planting

3 FLOWER BEDS x 2
At either end of terrace; mixed planting

4 DINING AREA
Table and chairs for six

5 WALLS AND STEPS
Walls double as seats

6 LAVENDER HEDGE
For year-round interest and fragrance

THE POTAGER

7 BRICK PATHS
The backbone of a traditional layout

8 OBELISKS x 4
Space-saving growing space

9 CENTRAL PARTERRE
Bay tree provides focal point

10 FRUIT AND VEGETABLE BEDS x 4
Crops to suit space available; stepover fruit trees line central paths

11 ARBOUR
With integrated bench seat

12 CUTTING GARDEN
Either side of arbour; flowers for cutting and espaliered soft fruit

13 BACK AND SIDE WALLS
Beds for fruit bushes

14 SCULPTURE
Feature and focal point

15 TOOL STORE/COMPOST AREA
Store could double as a potting shed; two compost bins for vegetable waste

Don't forget

Vegetables and fruit like to grow in a fairly sunny, sheltered site and need rich, well-drained soil. (*See also* pages 106–8.)

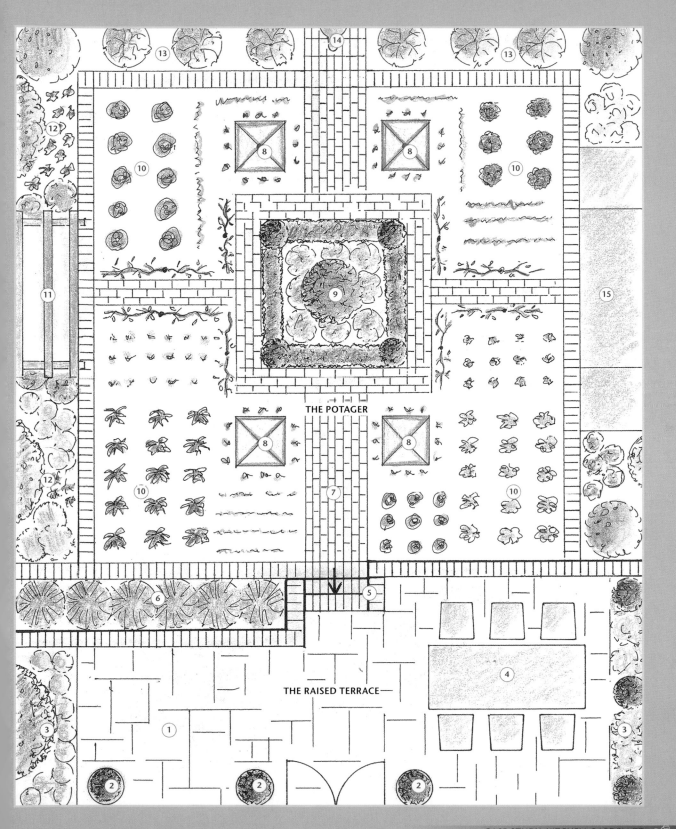

THE POTAGER

THE RAISED TERRACE

Plants for small gardens

Although the hard landscaping and permanent structures are important, in the end it is the plants and the way they're used that give a garden its character. Their form, colour and texture, their interaction with each other and their surroundings, and the way they change from day to day bring the space to life. In a small garden, it's particularly important to select your plants carefully as every plant really has to earn its keep.

Choosing and using plants

When choosing plants, try to avoid making the classic mistake of heading off to the garden centre and coming back with a trolley full of inappropriate plants that look great on the day but that don't suit the site, flower only fleetingly or don't work with neighbouring plants. Try to be methodical and plan properly and you'll save yourself a great deal of time, money and bother in the long run.

Doing your research

Get to know your garden well and read up on plants that will thrive in the conditions you find there; you're much more likely to have healthy plants if they're planted in the right place. Look in books or on the internet, and visit other small gardens for inspiration (*see* below).

Where to start

To plan a bed or border, draw up a scale drawing of the area, just as you would when you're designing the whole garden (*see* pages 64–6), and mark on it where the plants go. This can seem daunting if you don't know a lot about plants, but it will all fall into place if you do it

In this garden a yew hedge provides background structure while clipped box in containers make neat focal points along with other interesting features.

systematically, thinking of the major players first, followed by the supporting cast.

Structural and feature plants

First, decide on the plants that will make up the basic structure, or backbone, of the garden as well as the 'star' plants that will provide a strong focal point. These include trees, shrubs and architectural perennials. There are plenty to choose from (*see* pages 84–90).

Vertical planting

Next, think of the vertical dimension (*see* pages 92–6). Climbers and wall shrubs add height, colour and interest to the garden and take up very little space, so are ideal for a

small garden and invaluable in spaces where there is no garden to speak of, such as a courtyard.

The filler plants

Finally, think of the plants that you'll place between the structural and star plants and at the base of the climbers. These are usually the less permanent, often more colourful plants that are below eye level and consist of perennials, bulbs, annuals and biennials (*see* pages 99–104).

The Yellow Book

Every year the National Gardens Scheme produces a booklet of gardens that are open for charity. The gardens are usually only open for one or, at most, a few days a year so it is a real treat to be able to visit them, and a unique opportunity to see really small gardens, especially in towns. Any money made goes to charity.

Don't forget

In a small space there is nowhere for a poor performer to hide, so it's vital that every plant looks good. Only ever buy plants that are growing well and evenly with their branches or stems clad in healthy foliage.

Year-round interest

Try to include a variety of different plants that, together, will give you something to enjoy for 12 months of the year. At its most basic, this means including at least a few evergreens for year-round colour, but it's also important to pick plants with more than one season of interest, particularly where limited space means you can't fit all that many in. For example, choose something that has lovely flowers in spring and summer, attractive foliage, perhaps in autumn, and a pleasing shape for the rest of the time. Think about the types of plants that define the seasons and include something of each: bulbs for spring, annuals for summer, fruit and leaves for autumn, a distinctive form and evergreen foliage or interesting bark for winter.

Planting in layers

It's important to include a range of heights in your borders. Plants need to occupy three main spaces in a garden: the higher echelons (trees and climbers), the middle space (shrubs and taller perennials) and ground level (smaller perennials, annuals, biennials, ground cover and bulbs). By thinking about making a triangle or pyramid when you combine these, you'll ensure a good balance of sizes: for example, one tree at the apex, two or three shrubs or tall perennials in the middle and

five or more low-growing plants at the base. (*See also* page 15.)

The idea of building up multiple layers of plants is particularly important in a small garden, where every inch of space – up as well as across – should be used. Even in the tiniest garden, you can squeeze bulbs then annual bedding plants under and around perennials and shrubs, and lace climbers through larger plants to make the most of every patch of soil. Bulbs and annuals are also great for filling gaps in beds in spring and summer so, if possible, grow plenty in containers for slotting in wherever you need them. Once they've done their bit, pots of bulbs can be put out of sight again and annuals discarded.

Grouping plants

Most gardeners recommend grouping plants, especially the smaller ones, in threes, fives or more of the same type. This ensures they're conspicuous enough to play a part in the overall design when viewed from a distance – and groups of odd numbers are considered more natural-looking than even ones. Even in a small garden, it's often better to limit your choice of plants and have several of a few types to prevent a 'bitty' look. However, in a very tiny space, such as a courtyard or balcony, you could get away with having just one, since it's less likely to get lost in the crowd.

Dense, thoughtful planting from earth to sky ensures that this spot in the garden provides plenty to look at all year round.

This is a brilliant example of how repeating plants can work wonders: here, *Lavandula angustifolia* 'Hidcote' forms a soft frame for cushions of red-leaved *Berberis thunbergii* f. *atropurpurea* 'Atropurpurea Nana'.

Don't forget

Labels that say 'rampant', 'vigorous' or 'spreading' mean just that. Unless you have a specific purpose in mind, avoid using these plants in a small garden.

This lovely mature garden is full of plants and also includes a pergola and pool. The plants have enough space to grow and there is still plenty of room for the occupants. An attractive circular paving pattern adds interest at ground level.

Allow enough space

It may sound obvious, but the plants you pick should have sufficient space to grow, and not just when they're planted but for a few years afterwards at least. This is particularly important with larger plants such as trees and shrubs. The sizes given in books and on labels are usually indicators of how big the plant will be in five or so years. If you know its predicted height and spread, you can leave room for it to grow into and fill any

temporary gaps with short-term plants, such as annuals.

Small trees are often easier to accommodate in a small garden than large shrubs. Their slender trunks lift the branches a few feet off the ground so that other plants can be put around the base, and you and other garden users can move around them. Shrubs, on the other hand, tend to bush out from the ground, taking up much more room and allowing little in the way

of underplanting. Trees and shrubs that are suitable for a small garden are suggested on pages 84–91.

It's not just trees and shrubs that can get too big: be aware of smaller plants too. Some are well behaved and just fill the spot intended for them, but others quickly spread far and wide beyond your expectations.

Don't forget

Containers are useful for growing plants that prefer conditions other than your own. For example, rhododendrons, camellias, pieris and Japanese maples (*Acer palmatum*) prefer acid soil; if your soil is alkaline, you can use pots to give them what they need, rather than battling with your garden's natural conditions.

Combining colours and textures

Now for the arty bit – and here's the good news: there are very few rights and wrongs in combining plants. Depending on the look you want to achieve, almost anything goes. You could read ten books on garden design and come up with ten ways to plan your planting. All good garden designers have their own methods developed through years of trial and error; use the ideas here as a springboard to developing your own style.

Colour matters

Something that often worries people is how to choose colours that work together. The colour wheel (*see* page 14) is a good place to start, but in flowers and foliage there are myriad shades and a wealth of subtle colour combinations that can alter the effect. Begin by choosing just two plants that work well together, then select a third that looks good with one or the other of the first two, and build up from there. Aim for a selection of both complementary colours and contrasts, or clashes. Contrasts (opposites on the colour wheel) are much more obvious in a garden than complementary colours (adjacent on the colour wheel), so you don't need nearly as many of them to create an impression.

Blues and purples

Blues and purples are cool colours. They're gentle on the eye, and they encourage you to slow down and gaze at them in a leisurely way. The disadvantage of the darker shades is that they disappear into the shadows and at dusk, but use them with pale pinks or silvers to reduce this effect.

Pinks

Pinks can be warm and creamy or cool with a blue undertone. Creamy pinks are good background colours and go well with many other colours, while blue-toned pinks are dominant and ideal for creating strong colour combinations.

Reds and oranges

Reds and oranges are hot colours. They capture and hold your attention, even in tiny quantities. Use them in moderation to create splashes of colour and brighten up groupings that would otherwise be too subdued. Soft blues added to hot colour schemes will mellow colour clashes, while stronger blues produce a rich, saturated effect.

Yellows

Softer yellows make pleasing companions, while vivid yellows are good as contrasts and for bringing the scene to life. Sharp, pure yellows are eye-catchers. Like pink, yellow can be hot or cool. It's a good colour for warming up a blue and purple planting without losing the general air of sophistication, and its stronger shades are suitable for making reds and oranges more easily digestible.

Hot and cool colour combinations

There is plenty of fun to be had experimenting with foliage and flowers to find pleasing hot and cool combinations.

Hot red and orange: *Tulipa* 'Ballerina' and *Erysimum cheiri* 'Fire King'

Cool blues and purples: *Eryngium* x *zabelii* with *Stachys byzantina*

OTHER GOOD HOT COMBINATIONS

Bright pink and red-purple: *Lychnis coronaria* and *Cistus* × *purpureus*

Red, yellow and green: *Lobelia cardinalis* 'Queen Victoria' and *Canna* 'Striata'

Pink-orange and orange: *Echinacea* 'Art's Pride' and *Helenium* 'Moerheim Beauty'

Orange and yellow: *Dahlia* 'David Howard' and *Crocosmia* × *crocosmiiflora* 'Lady Hamilton'

OTHER GOOD COOL COMBINATIONS

Purple-pink and rich blue: *Anchusa azurea* 'Loddon Royalist' and *Allium giganteum*

Deep mauve (foliage) and purple-blue: *Rosa glauca* and *Perovskia* 'Blue Spire'

Silver (foliage) and white: *Artemisia* 'Powis Castle' *and Lavatera trimestris* 'Mont Blanc'

Creamy yellow and lavender blue: *Anthemis tinctoria* 'E.C. Buxton' and *Nepeta* 'Six Hills Giant'

The almost-black *Iris chrysographes* looks stunning set against a backdrop of fluffy fennel foliage.

The bold leaves of *Colocasia esculenta* 'Black Magic' complement the grassy foliage of *Arundo donax* var. *versicolor*.

Prickly *Eryngium giganteum* keeps its head above the flowing grassy *Hakonechloa macra* 'Aureola'.

Greens

Green is so predominant in gardens that it's tempting to discount it. However, depending on its shade, it can be effective alone in subtle schemes or for jazzing up flower combinations. Blue-greens and silver-greens are soft and cool, while lime greens and yellow-greens are sharper and more dominant.

Black and white

White is essentially a cool colour, although it acts like a hot one in that it stands out in the garden, especially at dusk. To avoid a 'spotty' look, position white-flowered plants so that they form a 'ribbon' through the flower bed.

True black is rare in a garden, but there are very deep shades of blue, red or purple which can have the same effect. Make the most of these dark colours by combining them with lighter shades of similar colours or by creating contrasts with lime green or yellow.

Shape and texture

Colour harmony is important, but you also need to make the most of plants' textures and habits when planning a garden (*see* pages 13 and 15). Successful shape combinations contribute to the rhythm of the garden, creating the right balance between movement and stillness. For example, an upright shrub teamed with mound-forming perennials produces a gentle deceleration in the flow around the space, while spiky perennials cause more of a sharp brake. Bun-shaped shrubs make a good full stop and a place to pause.

Texture will influence the effect of a plant's shape. In general, small leaves produce a busy, vibrant feel, while larger ones tend to be more restful. Combine several textures to ensure your planting is doubly interesting. Put soft leaves next to spiky ones, shiny ones with matt, and large with small.

Team plants with the hard landscaping

Look for ways to use plants to enhance hard landscaping in the garden (*see* pages 36–7). Soften hard paths with floppy mounds of foliage for an informal effect (*see* right), or echo them with upright, trained or architectural plants for a more contemporary look.

Remember you can paint walls, fences, trellis and other structures and can create contrasting colour effects with plants. For example, it's easy to warm up stark, white walls with red or orange flowers and cool down red-brick walls with mixtures of soft colours, especially creamy yellows and blues.

Structural and feature plants

Structural plants are important for two reasons: they form the backbone of the garden and they create focal points. Some, particularly evergreens, can perform both roles, while others are simply a foil for the rest of the planting. Try to select a good mixture of evergreens and deciduous plants for year-round interest and variety.

Structural plants are not necessarily tall; smaller specimens that have a distinct habit, leaf shape or colour can also be used to provide a structural element. The evergreen, shrubby box (*Buxus sempervirens*), for example, is often used to introduce a sense of formality and structure and is ideal for a small garden. However, even in the tiniest courtyard or balcony space, you do need to include at least one tallish plant, and preferably more. Tall plants draw your eye up and out into the world beyond and help to link the land with the sky. But at the same time, by growing up above our heads, they create a sense of enclosure, which increases our feelings of comfort and security.

Pittosporum tenuifolium 'Silver Queen' is a rounded shrub with shining leaves that create a soft effect.

Trees and tree-like shrubs

Small trees, neat evergreens and shrubs that can be pruned to be tree-like in outline are ideal structural plants for small gardens. Those that flower or have eye-catching features, such as interesting bark or foliage colour, make good star performers, while evergreens are particularly useful for full-time supporting roles.

Evergreen trees and tree-like shrubs

Large evergreen structural plants divide into two main groups: broad-leaved trees or shrubs, and conifers.

There is a wide choice of broad-leaved evergreens and many are excellent all-round performers for a small garden. Cultivars of *Pittosporum tenuifolium* are particularly useful. Most make large shrubs but they're easily trimmed back. 'Silver Queen' (*see* above) has a shimmering head of wavy leaves in silver and grey-green. 'Warnham Gold' has soft green leaves that turn golden yellow

Strong plant shapes underpin this formal, shady plot. Tall, clipped bays screen the seating area while spiky-leaved yuccas punctuate the far boundary.

in winter. 'Tom Thumb' has bronze-purple-flushed leaves and forms a small bush up to 1m (3ft).

The strawberry tree (*Arbutus unedo, see* right) is a beautiful specimen all year round, with white flowers and red, strawberry-like fruits. In winter it is valuable for its strong form, rich brown bark and evergreen, bay-like leaves. It can grow ultimately to about 10m (33ft) tall. 'Atlantic' is more compact and a better choice for small gardens. It is free-flowering and produces masses of fruits at the same time as the flowers in autumn.

Hollies also make good winter specimens, especially the variegated

Arbutus unedo is a hardworking evergreen structural plant with plenty of interest all year round.

The two-toned sculptural sprays of *Chamaecyparis obtusa* 'Nana Gracilis' brighten any garden.

More specimen trees and structural shrubs

FOR FLOWERS AND FRUIT
Cercis siliquastrum
Cornus 'Porlock'
Cotoneaster 'Hybridus Pendulus'*
Malus × purpurea 'Neville Copeman'
Malus × zumi 'Golden Hornet'

FOR FOLIAGE
Acacia baileyana 'Purpurea'*
Acer palmatum 'Shaina'
Acer shirasawanum 'Aureum'
Acer 'Silver Cardinal'
Cupressus sempervirens 'Totem Pole'*
Malus 'Directeur Moerlands'
Sorbus aria 'Lutescens'

GOOD STRUCTURAL CONIFERS
Chamaecyparis lawsoniana 'Ellwood's Gold'*
Chamaecyparis pisifera 'Boulevard'*
Cryptomeria japonica Elegans Group*
Juniperus chinensis 'Pyramidalis'*
Juniperus communis 'Hibernica'*
Picea pungens 'Fat Albert'*
Thuja plicata 'Fastigiata'*

*****evergreen**

fruiting varieties, such as cream-and-green *Ilex aquifolium* 'Silver Milkmaid' and gold-and-green *Ilex × altaclerensis* 'Lawsoniana', which has the added attraction of not being spiny. Both are shrubby trees that grow slowly to about 6m (20ft) tall, but can be kept smaller and bushier with pruning.

A well-chosen conifer can provide structure, a striking focal point and colour throughout the year. The secret of success is to choose one that doesn't grow too large and broad, as they take up a lot of space and can also drain the garden of water and nutrients, making it hard to establish other plants alongside.

The golden Irish yew, *Taxus baccata* Fastigiata Aurea Group, is slow-growing and very upright in habit, with narrow, deep-green leaves edged with gold. It makes an excellent exclamation mark on the corner of a bed, and a pair would be a good choice to emphasize an entrance, gateway or front door.

Thuja occidentalis 'Smaragd' is a narrow, tapering column of bright green foliage that would fit into any planting scheme. It grows slowly, to around 4m (13ft), is never greedy on space and casts little shade.

In minimalist planting schemes, perhaps in association with gravel, the cultivars of *Chamaecyparis obtusa* can be very effective and have an air of maturity from an early age. 'Nana Gracilis' (*see* above) has wonderful flattened and twisted sprays of emerald and dark green foliage that grow in various directions, creating a wonderfully sculptural effect.

Dwarf pines are also useful in this situation, with rocks, alongside paving and in containers. *Pinus mugo* has deep-green, bristly foliage on upright branches. The needles of the cultivar 'Winter Gold' turn rich gold in winter, striking in the winter sun and the perfect focal point amid dogwoods (*Cornus*) grown for their winter stems (*see* page 89) or winter-blooming heathers.

Don't forget

Many conifers, particularly the soft-leaved varieties, are much appreciated by birds for nesting and roosting sites.

Reminiscent of a willow, *Pyrus salicifolia* 'Pendula' has drooping, silver-green stems and leaves.

In autumn, the leaves of *Amelanchier lamarckii* turn shades of red and yellow, creating a fiery focal point.

This purple-leaved cultivar of *Acer palmatum* var. *dissectum* forms a soft mound of heavily cut foliage.

Deciduous trees and tree-like shrubs

Although evergreens are invaluable in a small garden, it is the deciduous trees and tree-like shrubs that often make the more striking contributions, simply because of the way they change with the seasons.

The white-barked silver birch (*Betula utilis* var. *jacquemontii*) is perhaps the most widely planted tree in gardens today. Although it appears light and airy as a young specimen, it grows to make a large, broad tree that is too big for many gardens. The natural habit of birches is ruined by pruning to control size, so choose a smaller-growing variety, such as 'Grayswood Ghost', which ultimately reaches 8m (26ft). An excellent focal point, it has emerald-green leaves, golden catkins in spring and pure white bark.

For a silver effect, *Pyrus salicifolia* 'Pendula' (*see* above) is a good choice. It has loosely weeping branches and narrow, silver leaves

that reflect the light. The branches are studded with creamy-white flowers in spring. Left to its own devices, it will form a loose, informal head and grow to 5m (16ft) in height. However, it responds well to pruning and can be shaped more formally and kept to 3m (10ft) high.

Everyone loves the snowy mespilus (*Amelanchier lamarckii, see* above), and for good reason. In spring, just as the bronze young foliage is opening, its upright, willowy branches are clothed with delicate white flowers. In autumn, the leaves turn red and yellow, and it may produce berries. Outstanding for structure in a small garden, it is also good placed among other plants for a more subtle effect.

With their delicate foliage and changing colours, few plants are more attractive than the Japanese maples. *Acer palmatum* 'Bloodgood' (*see* page 96) has five-lobed, wine-red leaves that turn rich scarlet in autumn. Fairly upright in habit, it

can reach 4m (13ft) high. There are low-growing varieties too – var. *dissectum* Dissectum Atropurpureum Group (*see* above) has finely cut leaves and is wider than it is tall. Most Japanese maples are excellent in containers and make good structural plants in a tiny space.

More trees for autumn and winter interest

AUTUMN FOLIAGE COLOUR
Acer japonicum
Acer palmatum 'Osakazuki'
Crataegus persimilis 'Prunifolia'
Euonymus europaeus 'Red Cascade'
Liquidambar styraciflua 'Worplesdon'
Pyrus calleryana 'Chanticleer'
Rhus typhina 'Tiger Eyes'

BEAUTIFUL BARK
Acer davidii 'George Forrest'
Acer griseum
Acer palmatum 'Sango-kaku'
Betula albosinensis 'Fascination'
Prunus maackii 'Amber Beauty'
Stewartia pseudocamellia

The polished mahogany-red trunk of *Prunus serrula* encourages interesting planting combinations.

A top-notch feature plant, *Catalpa bignonioides* 'Aurea' has a rounded head of bright yellow foliage.

Cercis canadensis 'Forest Pansy' has lovely foliage that can blend into a planting or make a classy focal point.

Trees with beautiful bark are especially valuable in winter. The Tibetan cherry (*Prunus serrula, see* above) has striking, shiny, deep-red bark, more than compensating for the small, short-lived white flowers. It makes a wonderful focal point and offers exciting planting possibilities underneath its light canopy.

Flowering cherries are popular, but their blossom can be a fleeting pleasure. The slender, upright *Prunus* 'Amanogawa' is a good choice for a narrow garden, taking up little space and clothed in double, pale pink

flowers from tip to toe in mid-spring. *Prunus* 'Ukon' deserves wider planting. It has ascending branches forming a vase-shaped head and an overall height of 5m (16ft). The new growth is pale copper in colour, the blossom creamy tinged with green and deep red, and in autumn the leaves turn rich gold and flame.

The flowering crabs, ornamental varieties of *Malus*, have the benefit of flowers in spring and attractive fruits in autumn. 'Evereste' is one of the finest for small gardens, with a cloud of white-and-pink, apple-blossom flowers in spring that are sweetly scented and loved by bees. The long-lasting, orange-yellow fruits can be used to make preserves if the birds don't get there first. The advantage of *Malus* over *Prunus* is that they can be pruned to control size and shape, like a fruiting apple.

With its yellow-green, mop-shaped canopy, the Indian bean tree (*Catalpa bignonioides* 'Aurea', *see* above) is striking. It has huge leaves,

reaches up to 6m (20ft), and bears bunches of white flowers in summer, followed by long seedpods.

Cercis canadensis 'Forest Pansy' (*see* above) is an excellent large shrub that fulfils the role of a tree. It has a spreading habit, with dark stems and large, heart-shaped, rich purple leaves that are shiny when young and velvety when mature. Tiny, purple-pink flowers appear on the bare branches in early spring.

Rowans (*Sorbus*) are among the most useful trees for a small garden, with divided foliage that often colours in autumn, white spring flowers and copious autumn berries. *Sorbus hupehensis* has white fruits, *Sorbus aucuparia* red and *Sorbus* 'Joseph Rock' yellow; *Sorbus vilmorinii* has white fruits that are pink when young. Rowans are on the small side, to about 10m (33ft); as they mature, their bare winter shape grows ever more distinguished.

Hawthorns (*Crataegus*) are also good all-rounders (*see* page 98).

Trees and shrubs for containers

Acer palmatum 'Taylor'
Ilex crenata 'Fastigiata'*
Juniperus communis 'Compressa'*
Musa (some*)
*Olea europaea**
Prunus incisa 'Kojo–no-mai'
*Trachycarpus fortunei**
evergreen

Pieris 'Forest Flame' has everything to make it a good structural plant and looks particularly striking in spring.

The flowers of *Choisya ternata* 'Sundance' can be sparse, but the glossy yellow foliage draws the eye.

An excellent low-growing shrub for evergreen structure, *Convolvulus cneorum* also has striking flowers.

Small and medium-sized shrubs

In a space that is not large enough to take a tree, medium-sized shrubs can provide height, while smaller ones are ideal for making low focal points and permanent structure.

Evergreen shrubs

Evergreen shrubs come in a range of shapes, sizes and foliage colours, and some have lovely flowers too. *Viburnum tinus* is a great all-rounder, valued for its late-winter to spring flowers and its tough constitution. 'Eve Price' is the most compact variety, ultimately reaching 3m (10ft). It is a reliable stalwart for shady corners, with its pink buds opening to white flowers followed by blue-black fruits.

Pieris 'Forest Flame' (*see* above) has bright red young leaves and fountains of white flowers. A slow-growing, upright evergreen shrub, it reaches 4m (13ft). *Pieris* need a lime-free soil, but make good shrubs for pots and are fine in shade. *Choisya ternata* has rich green leaves and

honey-scented white flowers in spring and again in summer and autumn. 'Sundance' (*see* above) has glossy, golden leaves. Both slowly form a compact bun shape up to 2.5m (8ft) wide. Himalayan honeysuckle (*Leycesteria formosa*) is a pretty, upright shrub with fresh grey-green leaves and hanging cords of white flowers surrounded by pink-red bracts through summer and early autumn, followed by red berries. *Convolvulus cneorum* (*see* above right) has pretty white flowers and hairy, grey-green leaves. It makes a small, neat focal point at the front of a border or raised bed.

Rosemary (*Rosmarinus*) and lavender (*Lavandula*) are both good structural plants with summer flowers. The strong, horizontal form of prostrate rosemary (*Rosmarinus officinalis* Prostratus Group) is eye-catching among upright neighbours, while 'Miss Jessopp's Upright' takes up little space on the ground. Lavenders are effective grown in groups or as low, informal hedges. Choose cultivars of *Lavandula*

angustifolia (*see* page 80) for their compact shapes and traditional lavender flowers. French lavender (*Lavandula stoechas*) has 'bunny ear' flowers and soft foliage.

The sun rose (*Cistus*) is another Mediterranean evergreen for a hot spot in the garden. It has large, saucer-shaped flowers, often pink and with striking markings. The white-flowered *Cistus* × *hybridus* is particularly useful because you can prune it to control its size.

A relatively new but superb variegated evergreen is *Skimmia*

More small and medium-sized shrubs

Aucuba japonica*	Hebe*
Berberis (some*)	*Leucothoe*
Buddleja	*fontanesiana*
Cotoneaster (some*)	*Osmanthus delavayi**
Daphne	*Philadelphus*
Deutzia	*Phlomis fruticosa**
Elaeagnus (some*)	*Ribes*
Euonymus (some*)	*Viburnum* × *juddii*
Fatsia japonica*	*Weigela*
Fothergilla major	*evergreen

Hedging plants

Hedges have various uses in the garden (*see* page 34). Evergreen hedges, such as box (*Buxus sempervirens*) and yew (*Taxus baccata*), are useful for year-round structure and topiary.

The spiny evergreen *Berberis darwinii* makes a good hedge, but the cultivars of the deciduous *Berberis thunbergii* are more exciting because of their coloured foliage. f. *atropurpurea* 'Rose Glow', for example, has white-flecked red leaves. When grown as a hedge, beech (*Fagus sylvatica*) retains its dead leaves until spring. Hawthorn (*Crataegus monogyna*) is a dense deciduous hedge, easily kept low and within bounds. For flowering hedges, choose a repeat-flowering rose such as 'Harlow Carr', or varieties of *Escallonia*. *Pittosporum tenuifolium*, with its shiny evergreen leaves, is also good.

For a different effect, consider bamboo hedging. Plant it with barriers to restrict its spread. Suitable bamboos for hedges include *Fargesia* species, *Phyllostachys aurea*, *Phyllostachys nigra* and *Pseudosasa amabilis*. Many grasses, particularly *Miscanthus* cultivars, and smaller shrubs (such as hebes) are useful for dividing up the garden and screening.

Sambucus racemosa 'Sutherland Gold' has yellow-green feathery foliage that creates a light effect.

Potentilla fruticosa cultivars make a lovely low hedge or can be used as feature plants. This is 'Grace Darling'.

japonica 'Magic Marlot'. It has cream-and-green foliage that looks good all year round, and domed clusters of white flower buds that appear in autumn, then turn deep red and finally open in spring to white, fragrant flowers. It is very compact (30cm/12in high), happy in shade and ideal for pots.

Deciduous shrubs

Deciduous shrubs change with the seasons, providing variety and interest over long periods and occasionally dropping out of the limelight to allow other plants to take the stage.

Very early and late performers, the witch hazels (*Hamamelis*) (*see* page 97) may be upright or spreading and have leaves that are similar to hazel, hence the common name. They bear

gorgeously scented, spidery late-winter flowers in yellow, orange or red and the leaves turn yellow or red in autumn.

Flowering slightly later, in late spring, *Exochorda* × *macrantha* 'The Bride' has frothy displays of white blooms. Also white, with arching sprays later in the season, is *Spiraea* 'Arguta'. Cultivars of *Spiraea japonica* are more compact, with white or pink flowers; the dwarf 'Goldflame' has pink flowers and yellow foliage.

The feathery foliage and soft, rounded forms of the ornamental elders are very striking. Place the wine-red *Sambucus nigra* f. *porphyrophylla* 'Eva' (formerly 'Black Lace') where its leaves will be backlit by the sun; *Sambucus racemosa* 'Sutherland Gold' (*see* above) makes its own sunshine. Both produce white and creamy-white flowers and black and red berries respectively.

For flowers in pink, blue or white there is little to beat the hydrangeas. With their large, glossy leaves, these bushy shrubs are excellent for subtle space-filling or as specimens. Their

flat or rounded heads of flowers last for many months, often fading through several shades, and finally become skeletal in the depths of winter. For the best blue flower colour, some need acid soil; most prefer moisture. Try *Hydrangea macrophylla* 'Zorro' for its black stems and flat, blue, lacy flowerheads.

Ideal for a dry spot with plenty of sunshine, the cultivars of *Potentilla fruticosa* are low-growing, shrubby plants with delicate, divided leaves and simple, round flowers in a range of colours, including white, pink, yellow, orange and red from spring to autumn. The flowers of 'Primrose Beauty' are creamy yellow and those of 'Grace Darling' (*see* above) pink fading to peach.

Excellent for winter interest are the dogwoods grown for their bright red and yellow stems. *Cornus alba* 'Elegantissima' is a good variety, with grey-green leaves edged white, as is the smaller-growing 'Sibirica Variegata'. Cut old stems back in late winter for bright-coloured new growth the following year.

Many euphorbias make good focal points when in flower. This is *Euphorbia characias* subsp. *wulfenii*.

Clumps of soft-leaved *Aruncus dioicus* form a lovely backdrop and are topped by white flowers in summer.

Valued for its glossy black canes, *Phyllostachys nigra* is a tall, structural plant – ideal in a jungle garden.

Perennials and grasses

Some large perennials make excellent structural plants. Those that are suitable for using as focal points are frequently referred to as architectural plants because they often have a striking form or particularly distinctive leaves. Evergreen perennials contribute all year round, while the herbaceous varieties are more ephemeral, but no less valuable. Although not always evergreen, grasses and bamboos are usually interesting most of the year.

Perennials

The evergreen *Euphorbia characias* subsp. *wulfenii* (see above) is a striking, stiff-stemmed, shrubby perennial with flashy, bright yellow-green floral bracts. It reaches 1.2m (4ft). Phormiums, also evergreen, can eventually spread rather wide but their colourful, strap-like leaves make interesting strong, upright shapes. Smaller types, to 1m (40in) tall and wide, include *Phormium* 'Jester' (pink

leaves with bright green edges) and 'Bronze Baby' (purple-bronze foliage).

The herbaceous *Aruncus dioicus* (see above) is happy in a damp, cool spot where it makes leafy clumps topped by white, feathery flowers in early summer. It reaches 2m (6ft).

Exotic perennials

Some tender plants, particularly cannas and bananas (*Musa* and *Ensete*), have large, glossy leaves that stand out among other less exotic plants because of their simple oval shapes. Some are also remarkable for their colours: those of *Canna* 'Striata' are acid yellow and green, while those of *Canna* 'Phasion' are purple and orange. *Ensete ventricosum* has green leaves with purple undersides and flushing. For more exotic plants, see page 109.

Grasses and bamboos

Bamboos are a must in a jungle garden, but their strong form also makes them suitable for structure in most gardens. The black-stemmed

Phyllostachys nigra (see above) and the yellow-stemmed *Phyllostachys aurea* 'Holochrysa' are both superb. Plant them in buried containers to restrict their spreading ambitions, or use them as screens. They are good in containers, so ideal for a small space, but need plenty of watering.

Many ornamental grasses are not evergreen but their white-brown flowerheads are decorative through the winter. The numerous cultivars of *Miscanthus sinensis* have a lot to offer: 'Flamingo' has fluffy pink flowerheads and golden autumn foliage; 'Morning Light' has narrow, white-edged leaves.

More architectural plants

Cynara cardunculus
*Dicksonia antarctica**
Eryngium giganteum
Miscanthus sinensis 'Gracillimus'
Silybum marianum
Stipa gigantea
*Verbascum olympicum**

**suitable for pots*

Neat plants for formal gardens

Slow-growing plants that keep their shape are a must for formal gardens, but even if you prefer an informal look, they can still find a place in your plans. Neat or shapely plants interspersed among more billowing forms instantly bring a sense of purpose to a flower bed or the whole garden. Their presence holds the structure together, enabling the other plants to be as fluid as they like.

Classic formal plants

Probably the most well known of all plants for formal spaces is box (*Buxus sempervirens*). It makes a large, bushy shrub if left unpruned, but is famed for its tolerance of pruning – into any number of shapes. The most frequently used cultivar is 'Suffruticosa', which is compact and slow-growing with green foliage, but forms with varying amounts of yellow in the leaves are also available. Other options are lavender (*Lavandula*), rosemary (*Rosmarinus*) and cotton lavender (*Santolina, see* below); there are compact or slow-growing cultivars of all of these and they can be trimmed to keep them neat.

The Italian cypress (*Cupressus sempervirens*) is ideal for a taller structural element; 'Green Pencil' (green) and 'Swane's Gold' (golden yellow) both reach about 6m (20ft) tall but only about 2m (6ft) wide at the most. An alternative is yew, which can

Low, neat hedging is good for creating a tidy frame into which you can plant almost anything to add interest.

① The blue, neat-growing *Iris pallida* and *Allium* 'Globemaster' look cool in this lush setting. *Hosta plantaginea* var. *japonica* provides bold foliage forms.

② Herb leaves and flowers in many shades of green and purple create a tapestry within this formal hedging.

be neatly pruned and has several narrow forms, including *Taxus baccata* 'Fastigiata', which is bright green, and 'Standishii', which is golden and reaches only 1.5m (5ft).

Neat growers

Traditionally, knot gardens were the epitome of formal-garden style, with low, clipped hedges framing beds filled with plants such as pinks (*Dianthus*), primroses (*Primula*) and violets (*Viola*), all popular due to their pretty daintiness. Herbs with relatively tidy habits, such as sage, rue and marjoram, were also common. Nowadays, formality can be more flexible. For a modern garden, widen the scope and include hostas, tulips and the softly hairy feathergrass (*Stipa tenuissima*), or for spiky contrasts, astilbes, heucheras,

irises and sisyrinchiums. All these are neat and self-contained, with attractive forms and flowers. Well-mannered annuals such as ageratum, busy lizzies (*Impatiens*), pelargoniums and French marigolds (*Tagetes*) add summer colour. To get neat formality without the trimming, pudding-bowl shaped hebes could be used instead of box: *Hebe cupressoides* 'Boughton Dome' is rich green and *Hebe* 'Pewter Dome' a glaucous grey-green.

Neat mounds of the cotton lavender *Santolina chamaecyparissus* 'Nana' have been used to create a formal pattern.

Vertical planting

Although valuable in all gardens, climbers and wall shrubs really come into their own in a small space. Most will grow on or along any vertical or horizontal surface, so can be used up walls and fences, as well as up and over a variety of decorative garden structures such as pergolas, arches and obelisks (*see* pages 23, 49–51 and right). Many are content to cling to or scramble through other plants in their race for the sky.

(*see* pages 23, 49–51 and right)

Golden hop (*Humulus lupulus* 'Aureus') is at its best in early summer, when its leaves are a brilliant acid green.

Using climbers and wall shrubs

Plants that are known for their vertical qualities are loosely separated into two groups: climbers and wall shrubs. Climbers usually have little in the way of a backbone and need something to lean against, while wall shrubs can quite easily stand alone but are often grown against a wall, usually to give them protection from cold. They tend to look better trained against a support as they produce a better display of flowers and stay neat and tidy.

As well as being suitable for training against structures, climbers can be grown through other plants, such as trees and shrubs, which allows you to make more of your restricted space.

Using evergreens

Since climbers and wall shrubs play a structural role, it makes sense to select some that will look good all year round. Luckily, there are plenty to choose from and as well as being evergreen, most have other points of interest such as flowers or berries. Evergreen climbers also create permanent cover where you want it, for example against a wall or fence, or a screen to provide privacy and a sense of enclosure. In dark spots, variegated ivies or euonymus provide a welcome brightness.

Climbers and wall shrubs for specific situations

PILLARS, OBELISKS, ARCHES AND COLONNADES
Clematis (most)
Lathyrus latifolius
Rosa 'Altissimo'
Rosa 'Golden Gate'
Rosa 'Warm Welcome'

STURDY PERGOLAS
Actinidia deliciosa
Campsis × *tagliabuana* 'Madame Galen'
Lonicera × *americana*
Rosa 'Madame Alfred Carrière'
Vitis vinifera
Wisteria floribunda
Wisteria sinensis

WARM, SUNNY WALLS
Actinidia kolomikta
Ceanothus (many*)
Cytisus battandieri 'Yellow Tail'*
Fremontodendron californicum
Jasminum officinale
Passiflora (most)*

COLD, SUNLESS WALLS
Cotoneaster horizontalis
Euonymus fortunei
Garrya elliptica
Hedera colchica 'Dentata Variegata'*
Hedera helix 'Glacier'*
Jasminum nudiflorum

*evergreen

Don't forget

Even if you need to cover the largest and ugliest of structures, don't invite the highly rampant Russian vine or mile-a-minute (*Fallopia baldschuanica*) into your garden.

Rosa 'Maigold' has loose, semi-double, bronze-yellow flowers in two flushes – early summer and autumn.

A bright, startling combination of *Pyracantha coccinea* and winter jasmine (*Jasminum nudiflorum*).

Clematis 'Madame Julia Correvon' and *Rosa* 'Dortmund' make a fiery, eye-catching partnership.

Yellow and gold

The evergreen winter jasmine (*Jasminum nudiflorum, see* above right) is valued for its bright yellow flowers in winter. However, it is sprawling and messy, so keep it under close control against a wall or fence.

The yellow-leaved golden hop (*Humulus lupulus* 'Aureus', *see* opposite) makes a wonderful foil to flowering climbers, particularly clematis, including 'Gipsy Queen' (purple-blue), 'Comtesse de Bouchaud' (pink, *see* page 95) and many others. Roses and clematis go well together too and are the classic climber combination. Yellow-flowered climbing roses include *Rosa* 'Maigold' (*see* above), which can be grown in shade, while *Rosa* 'The Pilgrim' is short and neat, with clear lemon-yellow flowers.

For evergreen yellow foliage the ivies are excellent. They are often more vigorous than the white-variegated ones (*see* page 94), but produce a warmer effect in a gloomy space. Try *Hedera helix* 'Buttercup', which is bright yellow and reaches 2m (6ft), or 'Midas Touch', which is tiny at 1m (40in); if you want to cover more space, 'Oro di Bogliasco' is green-and-yellow variegated and grows to 8m (26ft).

Red and orange

Evergreen and spiny, the firethorns (*Pyracantha, see* above) are valued for their long-lasting berries in gold, red or orange. These appear in autumn from white spring flowers. They're suitable against walls, as well as for hedging and screening.

For flowers in red or orange, choose a climbing rose. Their shades range from soft orange-apricot ('Schoolgirl') to a vibrant hot scarlet ('Dortmund', *see* above). If you want to pair them with similarly coloured clematis, 'Madame Julia Correvon' (*see* above) is one of the best of the blue-toned reds, while 'Rouge Cardinal' is scarlet. Orange clematis are rare, 'Vince Denny' being perhaps the closest.

Earlier in the year, Japanese quinces (*Chaenomeles*) have flowers in red, pink or white, followed by fruits. They flower on mature wood, so an annual restrictive pruning will improve the display. Most types are happy in a shady spot, but they will flower and fruit better in the sun.

Autumn colour for smaller walls

If you hanker after the glorious autumn shades of the Virginia creeper (*Parthenocissus quinquefolia*) or Boston ivy (*Parthenocissus tricuspidata*), but haven't got 15m (50ft) or more of spare wall, try their smaller, slow-growing relation *Parthenocissus henryana*, which eventually reaches 10m (33ft) and has toothed, green-purple leaflets that turn red in autumn. The ornamental grape *Vitis vinifera* 'Purpurea' (shown right with *Dicentra*) is also comparatively restrained, at just 7m (23ft), with rounded purple-red leaves that become even darker in autumn.

Two lovely climbers: *Solanum laxum* 'Album' with morning glory (*Ipomoea tricolor* 'Heavenly Blue').

Splashes of pale and dark grey-green and cream adorn the leaves of the restrained ivy *Hedera helix* 'Glacier'.

Ceanothus 'Concha' is smothered with dark blue flowers in late spring. It also has evergreen leaves.

White and cream

There is plenty of choice in both flowers and foliage if you're looking for climbers to give you white or cream. Jasmine (*Jasminum officinale*) is top of the list, with heavenly scented flowers. It's very vigorous, to 12m (40ft), but can be trimmed after flowering. A close second is the star jasmine (*Trachelospermum jasminoides*), which is evergreen and has similar flowers, but a less vigorous habit, reaching only 9m (30ft), and slowly. It isn't fully hardy, so is best in a sheltered spot, and it requires help to hang on to its support. *Solanum laxum* 'Album' (*see* above) only stands temperatures down to 0°C (32°F), but is such a refined plant that it's worth considering; it doesn't need much space and will reward you with fragrant flowers.

Don't overlook the ivies (*Hedera*). Many have white-variegated foliage in a range of shades, shapes and sizes. Unlike some green-leaved ivies, the variegated sorts are rarely thuggishly invasive, many are shade-tolerant and all are evergreen, so they're very useful for creating permanent brightness in a dark corner. Try the cultivars of *Hedera helix*, such as 'Adam', 'Glacier' (*see* above) and 'Minor Marmorata'.

Ideal for a tiny space, *Euonymus fortunei* 'Silver Queen' is another versatile plant that will grow as a bush or a wall shrub to 5m (16ft). It has oval, dark green, white-edged leaves and small white berries.

There are also many white climbing roses (*see* box, opposite) as well as some clematis.

Blue and purple

The vertical plant world is replete with blue- and purple-coloured flowers in a wide range of shapes, particularly clematis (*see* page 96).

Among the best-known blue wall shrubs are the California lilacs (*Ceanothus*). All are easy to keep under control against a wall and most have blue, honey-scented flowers; they do best in warmer regions. Choose an evergreen variety for year-round leaf cover. 'Concha' (*see* above) has red buds opening to dark blue flowers and

Rampant but worth it

There are a few climbers with such vigorous natures that they are difficult to contain. The two best known are wisteria (shown left) and *Clematis montana*. If you want to clothe a pergola or hide an unattractive shed, they will happily do the job. The clematis is so generous with its vanilla-scented flowers and the wisteria flowers are so beguiling that their rampant habits are easily forgiven and, in fact, both are controllable with a sensible pruning routine. Grapevines are another such problem; they are excellent for covering pergolas and arches and, if pruned carefully, will produce fruit, but beware: they are very fast-growing. Finally, for a cold north wall there is *Hydrangea anomala* subsp. *petiolaris*. It reaches 15m (50ft) and is robust, but elegant, with large, delicate sprays of white flowers in summer.

A clever pairing of flower form and colour, this is *Clematis* 'Multi Blue' with *Passiflora caerulea*.

These two different pinks make a great combination: *Rosa* 'New Dawn' and *Clematis* 'Comtesse de Bouchaud'.

The pink-splashed leaves of *Actinidia kolomikta* are excellent for disguising an ugly wall.

reaches 3m (10ft). Somewhat smaller (2m/6ft) are 'Pin Cushion' and *Ceanothus thyrsiflorus* 'Skylark', which have light blue and deep-blue flowers respectively. There are also pink- and white-flowered types.

For a more restricted space, there are several slender climbers that fit the bill. The chocolate vine (*Akebia quinata*) is more or less evergreen, with attractive, rounded leaflets of pale or blue-green. Hidden among the foliage in mid-spring, the dusky, dark purple flowers have a beguiling, spicy scent with hints of mint. This

Climbing roses

There are a huge number of climbing roses suitable for small gardens. Look for descriptions such as 'repeat-flowering', 'remontant', 'perpetual-flowering' and so on, all of which mean that the rose is good value in the flower department. Avoid rambler roses: these are generally much too vigorous for a small garden.

Excellent pink and white climbing roses include: 'Madame Alfred Carrière' (white), 'Alister Stella Gray' (creamy white), 'Compassion' (salmon pink), 'Iceberg' (white), 'James Galway' (deep pink), 'New Dawn' (*see* above right), 'The Generous Gardener' (warm pink).

plant runs along the ground if not tied to its support, but it eventually becomes woody and then will happily stay in place. The Chilean potato tree *Solanum crispum* 'Glasnevin' is slightly hardier than *Solanum laxum* (*see* opposite), with deep-purple to blue fragrant flowers from summer into autumn. This is a fast-growing climber to 6m (20ft), which makes it good for filling a gap.

The flowers of the passionflower (*Passiflora*) are justly admired, with their prominent central bosses. *Passiflora caerulea* (*see* above left) is among the hardiest, with white flowers, made blue by their dense circle of central filaments. If you're lucky it will also produce orange fruit, which are edible but not particularly tasty. This is a vigorous plant with plenty of leafy growth, but can be hard pruned.

Pink

The genus that contains the kiwi fruit (*Actinidia*) also includes one of the most extraordinary climbers, with leaves that look as if they have

been dipped into not one, but two paint pots: they are rich green with both pink and white markings. Called *Actinidia kolomikta* (*see* above), this twining plant grows to 5m (16ft) or more and has tiny, fragrant white flowers and (if you have both male and female plants) edible fruit.

The common honeysuckle cultivars *Lonicera periclymenum* 'Belgica' and 'Serotina' (*see* page 97) have flowers in pink and purple in mid- and late summer. They're lovely, but can be untidy in habit. Train them across an arch or pergola, where their scent can be enjoyed, and intertwine them with clematis, roses and other climbers to extend the season of interest.

Good pink clematis include the vigorous 'Comtesse de Bouchaud' (*see* above left) and the more restrained 'Hagley Hybrid'. Pink climbing roses are available in vast numbers and many make great garden plants. 'Constance Spry' is an old favourite, while 'The Generous Gardener' is quite new and thornless.

Combining climbers with other plants

Some climbers have a spectacular but very brief flowering season. However, by growing them through established trees and shrubs, as well as teaming them with each other, you will ensure maximum impact in a small garden.

Clematis are particularly useful in this respect and will scramble almost anywhere, allowing you to experiment with all sorts of colour combinations (*see* right). Annual climbers are also good for this (*see* below right) and, since they die off at the end of the growing season, there is less risk of them swamping their host than with some perennials.

Combining more than one climber on a structure is a classic way to extend the period of interest as well as to hide bare stems and fill in gaps. Roses and clematis are a deservedly popular pairing; as well as growing very well without restricting or swamping each other, their flowers are incredibly beautiful together.

The pale blue flowers of *Clematis* 'Prince Charles' (left) draw out the blue tones in the foliage of the Japanese maple *Acer palmatum* 'Bloodgood' (right).

For a sizzling contrast, pair the clean, sharp colours of *Clematis* 'Polish Spirit' (left) and the smoke bush *Cotinus coggygria* 'Golden Spirit' (right).

OTHER GOOD COMPANIONS

Clematis alpina (blue) with *Taxus baccata* 'Standishii' (golden leaves)

Clematis 'Bill MacKenzie' (yellow) with *Eccremocarpus scaber* (orange-red)

Clematis × *durandii* (indigo-blue) with *Lonicera nitida* 'Baggesen's Gold' (cream)

Clematis 'Étoile Violette' (violet-purple) with *Trachelospermum jasminoides* (white)

Clematis henryi (white) with *Ceanothus* 'Concha' (dark blue), *see page 94*

Clematis 'Perle d'Azur' (blue) with *Parthenocissus henryana* (red in autumn)

Climbers such as clematis can become leggy at the base. Here, achilleas and cornflowers cover up the stems.

Remember to plant around the lower stems of climbers, as these plants often become somewhat thin at the base as they age. Add bulbs, annuals and a variety of small perennials for a longer season of interest.

Annual climbers

Cobaea scandens (cup-and-saucer vine)*

*Eccremocarpus scaber**

Ipomoea lobata (Spanish flag)*

Ipomoea tricolor (morning glory)*

Lathyrus odoratus (sweet pea)*

*Rhodochiton atrosanguineus**

Thunbergia alata (black-eyed Susan)*

Tropaeolum majus (nasturtium)*

Tropaeolum peregrinum (Canary creeper)*

suitable for pots

Fragrant plants

Small, sheltered gardens are ideal for fragrant plants, since their perfume lingers and is more intense. If your garden is exposed, prevent the scent from being wafted away by creating sheltered spots using screens or other plants. Paths and steps are good sites for perfumed plants, as are pergolas and arches, of course – anywhere you regularly pass by or where you sit.

Winter and spring

There is no shortage of scented flowers that open from late winter to welcome the spring; even some species of the snowdrop (such as *Galanthus elwesii*) have a delicate fragrance. Among shrubs, one of the best performers is *Daphne odora* 'Aureomarginata'. This starts opening its small, purple-white flowers in late winter and the generous scent is divine. Witch hazels (*Hamamelis*) also have a perfume that pervades the air on still mornings. The evergreen Christmas box (*Sarcococca confusa*) has exquisitely fragrant, whiskery, white flowers.

Many of the multi-flowered daffodils have gorgeous scents and can be grown in pots to tuck in among other plants. Often flowering on the cusp of early summer, tulips are not famous for their scent. However, some have a honey perfume, including 'Generaal de Wet' (rich orange) and 'Bellona' (golden yellow). Grow them with wallflowers (*Erysimum*), which are colourful and highly scented.

Smell is our most evocative sense. Make the most of it by filling your garden with fragrance.

① Honeysuckle (*Lonicera periclymenum* 'Serotina') enhances many a summer evening.

② Crisp spring mornings are the best time to appreciate *Hamamelis* × *intermedia* 'Diane'.

③ Mock oranges (*Philadelphus*) have a heady, intoxicating perfume.

④ The subtle fragrance of *Amaryllis belladonna* is strongest on balmy autumn days.

Plants with aromatic foliage

Aloysia citrodora (lemon verbena)*
Artemisia (wormwood)*
Lavandula (lavender)*
Pelargonium (scented-leaf geranium)*
Rosmarinus officinalis (rosemary)*
Salvia (sage)*
Thymus (thyme)*
*suitable for pots

Summer

From the intoxicating mock oranges (*Philadelphus*) to the sweet, coconut-ice perfume of night-scented stock (*Matthiola bicornis*), summer is full of fragrance. The following scented annuals are good for a tiny garden: alyssum (*Lobularia*), cherry pie (*Heliotropium*), mignonette (*Reseda*), tobacco plants (*Nicotiana*), petunias, sweet peas (*Lathyrus odoratus*) and stocks (*Matthiola*).

Among permanent plants, roses (*Rosa*), honeysuckle (*Lonicera*) and lilies (*Lilium*) are obvious choices for their perfumes. For something subtler, try the chocolate plant (*Cosmos atrosanguineus*) – yes, it's chocolate scented! – and peppery lupins; and, in a sunny spot, old-fashioned pinks (*Dianthus*) for their clove scent.

Autumn

Fragrance becomes rarer in the autumn, although roses and many annuals will continue to flower if the weather is kind. *Cyclamen hederifolium* has a sweet fragrance. Grow it in pots that you can lift up closer to nose level so it's easier to smell the lovely flowers. Also, the pink trumpets of *Amaryllis belladonna* are beautifully scented. A good choice for a jungle garden is the half-hardy ginger lily *Hedychium gardnerianum*, which has spires of scented yellow flowers.

Plants to encourage wildlife

Despite our increased understanding and concern about what birds, small mammals and insects need to survive, these creatures are still suffering from loss of habitats, making it ever-more important that our gardens provide a haven for them. This doesn't mean your garden has to be wild – even the tidiest garden can attract, feed and shelter wildlife if you choose the right plants.

Trees and shrubs

Most hawthorns (*Crataegus*) are attractive to birds and bees because of their late-spring flowers and red autumn berries. *Crataegus monogyna*, the common species, is thorny and fast-growing with white, talc-scented flowers. It cares little where it grows and can be trimmed to keep it tidy. Rowans (*Sorbus*) are good all-rounders for wildlife (*see* page 87), while shrubby cotoneasters buzz with bees in spring and the birds eat the berries through the winter. Choose compact varieties such as 'Hybridus Pendulus' and *Cotoneaster horizontalis*.

Butterflies love buddleias, which in summer have fragrant, cone-shaped flowerheads in blues, pinks and purples. Some forms can be rather unshapely and are not ideal for a tiny space but few mind a good pruning in spring. If you prefer neater shrubs, try the smaller hebes including *Hebe macrantha* and *Hebe* 'Hagley Park' or one of the many flowering heathers.

Bulbs, annuals and perennials

Many bulbs, perennials and annuals produce nectar- and pollen-rich flowers that provide food for insects. In winter and spring, the snowdrops (*Galanthus*) stand a meal for any precocious bees, and a little later bugle (*Ajuga reptans*) and lungwort (*Pulmonaria*) are popular. Columbines (*Aquilegia*) are in evidence in late spring and early summer and they give way to annuals, for example snapdragons (*Antirrhinum*), cherry pie (*Heliotropium*) and the highly aromatic marigolds (*Tagetes*). Perennials such as catmint (*Nepeta*), evening primrose (*Oenothera*) and penstemons should not be forgotten, nor should the ice plants (*Sedum spectabile*) and single-flowered asters, particularly as they continue flowering late into autumn.

Herbs

Herbs are very important plants for bees and other insects and range from the shrubby hyssop, rosemary and

If you want to help insects, such as bees, grow a range of flowering plants.
① Bees and butterflies love sedums, especially those that flower in autumn.
② Pink columbine (*Aquilegia*), alliums and feathery fennel look great and provide a buffet for beneficial insects.

lavender, to the diminutive thymes and occasionally thuggish mints (plant them in sunken pots to keep them in check). Feverfew (*Tanacetum*) is another to consider, as are chives.

More plants for wildlife

PLANTS FOR NECTAR AND POLLEN
Anethum graveolens (dill)*
Delphinium
Digitalis (foxglove)*
Echinops ritro (globe thistle)
Eryngium giganteum (sea holly)
Foeniculum vulgare (fennel)*
Helianthus annuus (sunflower)*
*Verbena bonariensis**

BERRYING PLANTS
Berberis (most)
Ilex (holly)
Lonicera periclymenum (honeysuckle)
Pyracantha (firethorn)
Viburnum (many)
suitable for pots

With lots of berries and attractive foliage in autumn, *Crataegus persimilis* 'Prunifolia' is good for decoration and wildlife.

Don't forget

Simple, single flowers are the best choice for bees and other insects. Semi-doubles and doubles often do not produce nectar.

Filler plants

The fillers are the plants that go in between the structural plants and under the climbers. Although many do have attractive leaves and some are grown purely for their foliage, the main reason for choosing the majority of them is their flowers. Fillers may remain in the garden for a long time, but they are far more easily shifted and experimented with than the key structural plants, and this means they can be more fun.

Filler choices

Fillers belong to one of four main plant groups: perennials, bulbs, annuals and biennials. Perennials are divided into herbaceous types, most of which die down to the roots in winter, and evergreen types, which have some leaves all year round. The majority of bulbs produce fresh leaves and flowers each year, dying down in between times. The word 'bulb' is often used for other plants with fleshy roots, such as corms, tubers and rhizomes. Annuals and biennials are usually grouped together, since their life cycle is quite similar. Annuals grow, flower and die in the same year, while biennials need a winter in between growing and flowering.

Using fillers

When you're faced with a new flower bed full of nothing but bare earth, it can be difficult to know where to start. There will probably be plenty of plants you like and want

It takes some careful planning, but it is possible to have flowers in bloom providing wonderful splashes of colour all summer long, even in a small space.

to include, but how do you decide where to put them? A good way to start is to think of the space in terms of the seasons. For example, a flower bed or container close to the house is a good place to focus on creating a great display in late winter and early spring, as this is the bed you'll see most of from inside the house; one next to the patio or your favourite bench ought to be full of flowers in summer.

Another planning strategy is to focus on colour-themed borders. For instance, you could put cool colours in a shady part of the garden and hot ones in full sun, or you might decide to have a border devoted to white plants or blue ones.

Next, flesh out your plans by thinking in terms of short bursts of excitement coupled with longer periods of subtle display. What you're aiming for is a selection of structural plants that provide substance for much of the year (see pages 84–90) and then some brighter, more colourful stars that enjoy short-term celebrity status before fading away again. This produces a balanced result and means that you have something to look at most of the time.

Don't forget

Make full use of containers to fill gaps and dull periods with temporary flower displays (see pages 52–5).

Red emerging stems of a peony provide the perfect foil for the soft yellow of primroses (*Primula vulgaris*).

Sharp, acid-yellow *Hakonechloa macra* 'Aureola' and pale blue *Muscari azureum* look good in a spring border.

Spring filler plants

Bulbs are the brightest source of spring colour, but there are also plenty of colourful perennials around now too.

White and yellow

Snowdrops (*Galanthus*) are among the best spring bulbs. The common snowdrop (*Galanthus nivalis*) is small and delicate, while *Galanthus elwesii* is taller with wide leaves and *Galanthus* 'S. Arnott' is more strongly scented. Daffodils (*Narcissus*) are also useful for a small garden. There is great variation in the flowering period, sizes and colours of daffodils, so choose carefully. The dwarf ones are often best, particularly 'Jack Snipe' (white and yellow), 'Jenny' (white and lemon yellow), 'Jetfire' (yellow and orange) and 'Tête-à-Tête' (golden).

If you have a shady garden, *Anemone nemorosa* is an excellent choice, with buttercup-shaped, white flowers (blue in some varieties). It goes beautifully beneath a silver birch. For a soft yellow in a similar location, there is nothing to beat our lovely native primrose (*Primula vulgaris*, *see* above left).

Blues, purples and pinks

Crocuses are much in evidence in spring. The Dutch crocus (*Crocus vernus*) is available in many blue and purple shades, including rich violet

('Purpureus Grandiflorus') and pale purple ('Vanguard'), which combine well with small daffodils. Of similar size are the starry blue flowers of *Chionodoxa* and *Scilla*, both of which are bright and delicate and available in white too. The grape hyacinths (*Muscari*) are sturdier, with flowers ranging from dark purple to pale blue; *Muscari azureum* (*see* left) is pale, while *Muscari latifolium* has two shades on each spike. Much more delicate are the elfcap-like flowers of the barrenworts (*Epimedium*). Most have bronze young foliage and bright autumn colours too. Dog's-tooth violets (*Erythronium*) also have attractive wide, spotted leaves that complement their hanging bells in many shades, including pinks and purples. Lungworts (*Pulmonaria*) have tiny flowers in blue or pink. Many also have decorative silver-spotted foliage. Some hellebores, such as *Helleborus × sternii*, have

More plants for spring

Anemone blanda (wood anemone)
Bergenia (elephant's ears)
Brunnera macrophylla 'Jack Frost'
Eranthis hyemalis (winter aconite)
Fritillaria meleagris (snakeshead fritillary)
Hyacinthus (hyacinth)
Iris 'Harmony'
Iris 'Joyce'
Polygonatum × hybridum (Solomon's seal)
Primula (many)
Trillium
Trollius

The pale pink flowers of a hellebore (*Helleborus × hybridus*) overtop the richer pink blooms of *Cyclamen coum*.

silvery foliage, but most are grown for their nodding flowers in purple, pink, cream and green. Cyclamens have pretty flowers (*Cyclamen coum* in spring and *Cyclamen hederifolium* in autumn) and lovely foliage.

Summer filler plants

If spring is full of colour, summer is overflowing with it. The abundance of summer flowers means you should be able to find plenty to fill every space in the garden.

Blues and purples

Flowers in cool blues and purples, blue-pinks and dark mauves often belong to the more sophisticated garden-dwellers, such as alliums (*see above* right), delphiniums and Jacob's ladder (*Polemonium*). All these have a long season of interest in flower, form and foliage, and generally tidy habits – all of which make them excellent choices where

Silver-blue and purple-red are complementary: this is *Eryngium × zabelii* and *Allium sphaerocephalon*.

The silver leaves of *Artemisia ludoviciana* 'Valerie Finnis' reveal silvery tints in *Achillea millefolium* 'Cerise Queen'.

space is at a premium. The flower spikes of larger delphiniums will need support, and the leaves of many alliums die before the flowers appear and look a bit messy, so these slender bulbs are best squeezed in among other plants rather than planted in groups on

their own. More rarely seen, but with equally lovely flowerheads in rich blue, is *Triteleia laxa*.

Annuals are often garish, but there are some with more restraint that could be used to augment a cool display. They include ageratums, love-in-a-mist (*Nigella, see* page 102) and pastel busy lizzies. Some cultivars of the field poppy (*Papaver rhoeas*) have lovely soft watercolour shades.

Shades of pink

Varying from soft pastels to strong magentas, pink can be cool, warm or hot. Cool pinks are found in such plants as bleeding heart (*Lamprocapnos spectabilis*, formerly *Dicentra*), *Mimulus naiandinus* and the tiny, spreading London pride (*Saxifraga × urbium*). The saxifrages, most of which are very small, are all well worth exploring for their variety of foliage, form and colour. Hotter pinks include *Gladiolus communis* subsp. *byzantinus* and *Erodium manescavii*, which would win prizes for their vividness were it not for the

Using slender and see-through plants

Some magical effects can be achieved by using plants that are tall but slender, allowing you to see something of what lies beyond them. Because you can choose to focus on them or look through them, they seem to create another dimension and certainly increase the sense of depth in any planting. Almost in contradiction, these plants can also create a feeling of enclosure and privacy without adding bulk, weight or shade.

Aconitum (monkshood)
Anethum graveolens (dill)
Cosmus bipinnatus
Crambe cordifolia
Delphinium
Deschampsia flexuosa 'Tatra Gold'
Eremurus (foxtail lily)
Foeniculum vulgare (fennel)
Gypsophila paniculata
Limonium platyphyllum
Linaria purpurea 'Canon Went'
Perovskia 'Blue Spire'
Stipa gigantea (golden oats)
Thalictrum delavayi
Verbascum
Verbena bonariensis (left)
Veronica spicata
Veronicastrum virginicum

A timeless and beautiful pairing of bright, fresh-green bells of Ireland (*Moluccella*) and rich-blue love-in-a-mist (*Nigella*).

Dotted among cow parsley in this striking informal planting are the intriguing, almost black flowers of *Scabiosa atropurpurea* 'Chile Black'.

hardy geraniums, which are often even brighter. Not all geraniums are pink though, and in the summer garden they are among the most versatile plants – available in a range of sizes from minute to billowingly large. Even when not in flower, their mounds of deeply cut foliage are a perfect foil for other blooms.

The pincushion white or crimson flowerheads of *Astrantia major* are carried above deeply cut leaves from early summer. It does particularly well in damp spots. For a drier situation, the fleabanes (*Erigeron*) are a good choice. Although the small-flowered *Erigeron karvinskianus* is perhaps best known, it can be an enthusiastic self-seeder and there are others worth considering, such as 'Charity' (pale lilac), 'Gaiety' (rich pink) and 'Quakeress' (pink-white).

Many sedums (*see* opposite) start to bloom in late summer and on into autumn, their flowerheads and succulent foliage providing colour and strong forms.

Green

Green can be more than just a background colour and makes a good choice for a colour-themed flower bed. All greens go together well – there is a huge variety of shades – and there are plenty of plants with green flowers as well as foliage. Green is a restful colour, but for something more arresting you need only a splash or two of other colours or choose some variegated

plants that will add subtle white or golden-yellow tints (*see* page 105).

Lady's mantle (*Alchemilla mollis*) is among the best known of green plants. Another cottage-garden favourite, bells of Ireland (*Moluccella laevis, see* far left) is an annual with pale green leaves and tiny, white fragrant flowers surrounded by large green bracts. *Nicotiana langsdorffii*, also annual, is tall at 1.5m (5ft) with green tubular flowers, while *Nicotiana* 'Lime Green' reaches only 60cm (2ft). The soft plumes of feathergrass (*Stipa tenuissima*) remain green late into the year. For a touch of acid yellow, include the biennial *Smyrnium perfoliatum* or the autumn-flowering red-hot poker *Kniphofia* 'Percy's Pride'.

White and black

There is something undeniably appealing and sophisticated about a white garden. If you like the idea, you could devote a flower bed to white or create a secluded white 'room'. Wonderful whites can be found among plants that produce solid-looking flowers like lilies,

Using dark plants for effect

You can create stunning colour combinations with dark plants. Here, a rich purple-leaved heuchera sets off the violet spires of salvia and contrasts with a backdrop of silvery artemisia. Alternatively, try the snapdragon *Antirrhinum majus* 'Black Prince' with a dark cornflower like *Centaurea cyanus* 'Black Boy'. For something more shocking, add an orange of the sort found in pot marigold (*Calendula officinalis* 'Orange King') and soften the lot with *Pennisetum setaceum* 'Rubrum', which is a fluffy purple-red grass.

leucanthemums and cosmos, as well as more ephemeral gypsophilas, nicotianas and astilbes. Consider adding some silver-leaved plants, too; *Anaphalis triplinervis* is good and there are plenty of suitable artemisias.

White may be all about innocence and purity, but black is the epitome of class. Near-black flowers include *Scabiosa atropurpurea* cultivars, including 'Chile Black' (*see* opposite), and *Alcea rosea* 'Nigra'. Try framing them with warmer colours and paler ones to avoid a funereal effect.

Red and orange

There is rarely anything subtle about flowers in strong reds and oranges. Even in the smallest numbers they make their presence felt, drawing your eye to them over and above everything else. If you like such boldness, make sure you add some hot colours to your garden.

For earlier in the season, select a poppy, such as *Papaver orientale* Goliath Group 'Beauty of Livermere'. Or, for a mixture of oranges and yellows, pick the Iceland poppy *Papaver nudicaule* var. *croceum* 'Flamenco', or the annual California poppy (*Eschscholzia californica*). Peonies are available in bright reds, as are gladioli and penstemons.

Bright-coloured annuals	
Clarkia	Nicotiana*
Cosmos bipinnatus	Papaver rhoeas
Dianthus barbatus	Shirley Group
	(field poppy)
Diascia*	Petunia*
Impatiens (busy	Tagetes*
Lizzie)*	Verbena × hybrida*
Malcomia maritima	Zinnia*
(Virginian stock)	
Mimulus*	*suitable for pots

Sedum telephium Atropurpureum Group has purple flowers and foliage that soften the impact of the orange-red *Dahlia* 'Tally Ho'.

Dahlias are often the first stop for hot-coloured plants and include some of the brightest reds and oranges, which are welcome in late summer and early autumn. Try the ever-popular 'Bishop of Llandaff' (*see* below) or 'Tally Ho' (*see* above) for red and 'David Howard' for orange; all three have rich maroon foliage. Flowering at around the same time

are the crocosmias (montbretia); 'Lucifer' has the reddest flowers.

If you want heat in a hurry, look no further than pelargoniums (commonly but incorrectly known as 'geraniums'). For floral display and variety, they are head and shoulders above most other hot-coloured bedding plants.

Yellow

Yellow often comes with daisy-like flowers, and throughout summer *Anthemis tinctoria* cultivars produce these in all shades of yellow, from palest yellow ('Sauce Hollandaise'), to pale lemon ('E.C. Buxton') and clear yellow ('Kelwayi'). Many daylilies (*Hemerocallis*) have yellow flowers, either star-shaped or more rounded and all gorgeously opulent, while *Achillea filipendulina* 'Gold Plate' (*see* below) is not to be missed for its sun-yellow, flying-saucer flowerheads. It gets rather tall (1.5m/5ft); *Achillea* 'Coronation Gold' is better for a confined space, but less impressive.

This striking planting blends the flat flowerheads of *Achillea filipendulina* 'Gold Plate' with red *Dahlia* 'Bishop of Llandaff'. The striped canna leaves create vertical accents.

Rudbeckia fulgida var. deamii has strong yellow flowers, softened here by gentle lilac-blue Aster azureus.

Purple Verbena rigida furnishes the bare stems of Nerine bowdenii with fern fronds completing the picture.

Autumn and winter filler plants

If you've chosen your structural plants and climbers and wall shrubs well you should have some colour in autumn and can add to this with filler plants.

Colourful flowers

Among the brightest of autumn flowers are the asters (see above). They are well known for their in-your-face pinks, but there are sophisticated blues and whites, too. The flowers range from tiny and single to large pompons: 'Little Carlow' is a small-flowered blue; 'Photograph' has sprays of pale lavender, and Aster novae-angliae 'Andenken an Alma Pötschke' is large and cerise-pink. Asters last a season or two in pots but generally do much better in the ground.

Autumn crocus (Colchicum autumnale) and the taller Nerine bowdenii (see above right) are best planted in a sunny site. Both have bright pink flowers; those of the crocus appear without leaves, which start to grow in spring.

Heleniums supply orange-red and yellow in warm, rusty shades, as do bedding chrysanthemums and dahlias. Helenium 'Moerheim Beauty' is very popular, with coppery-red flowers; 'Wyndley' is yellow with orange tints. In mild autumns, canna lilies (see page 109) make a long-lasting contribution with flowers and leaves.

Autumn also brings rudbeckias, with daisy flowerheads. Rudbeckia hirta 'Prairie Sun' is a real stunner, with soft yellow, pale green-centred flowers; many other cultivars are available in yellows and rusty orange in a range of heights, including dwarf. Rudbeckia fulgida var. deamii, with black eyes, is also striking (see far left).

Decorative seedheads

Although the flowers of many filler plants start to deteriorate with the colder, longer nights of autumn, their seedheads continue to decorate the garden often until the following spring, fading to pale brown and white as they age. Grasses such as miscanthus and stipa are often quoted as having excellent seedheads, and indeed they do, but other grasses, including festucas (Festuca glauca cultivars), panicums and pennisetums, are equally attractive.

It is tempting to wax lyrical about other seedheads: those of opium poppy (Papaver somniferum) are often likened to pepperpots, while love-in-a-mist (Nigella damascena) has puffed-up seedheads, striped like miniature hot-air balloons. Never be too quick to tidy up the flower bed – seedheads can be an unexpected joy.

More plants with decorative seedheads

Acaena microphylla 'Kupferteppich'*

Briza maxima

Foeniculum vulgare (fennel)*

Helianthus annuus (sunflower)*

Lagurus ovatus (hare's-tail grass)

Lunaria annua (honesty, left)

Sedum spectabile (ice plant)*

Selinum wallichianum

**suitable for pots*

Foliage plants

Foliage is part of every garden and is particularly useful for providing interesting textures and forms (*see* page 83). It is tempting to choose plants only for their flowers, but the leaves are around for very much longer and so, in reality, can make a more important contribution to the overall success of the garden. Many plants are grown mainly for their leaves, even those that also produce attractive flowers.

Hostas

Among foliage plants, hostas are probably the most prized. Their pointed oval leaves come in a range of sizes, from around 5cm (2in) long in *Hosta gracillima* to 50cm (20in) or more in *Hosta* 'Sum and Substance'. The foliage is variously coloured and variegated with shades of blue-green, yellow and white, and they also produce tall summer flower spikes. They are best in damp soil and shade.

Ferns

Ferns also make excellent architectural plants in shady sites. Their forms are attractive but soft, and change with the seasons. In spring, the unfurling fronds are soft green or bronze and go well with bulbs. In summer, their feathery shapes can merge into the

Leaves are every bit as interesting as flowers. Their shapes, sizes, colours and textures vary enormously.

① A wavy-edged form of hart's tongue fern (*Asplenium scolopendrium*) mingles with silvery cyclamen leaves.

② Blue fescue (*Festuca glauca*) comes in many varieties. This beautiful glaucous one is called 'Elijah Blue'.

③ This dramatic foliage planting, with strong horizontal lines, includes from the bottom: *Hosta* 'Halcyon'; *Iris pseudacorus* 'Variegata'; *Rodgersia podophylla*; *Polygonatum* × *hybridum*.

Variegated plants

Arabis alpina subsp. *caucasica* 'Variegata'

Astrantia major 'Sunningdale Variegated'*

Aubrieta 'Aureovariegata'*

Erysimum 'Walberton's Fragrant Star'

Erythronium (many)*

Farfugium japonicum 'Aureomaculatum'*

Hosta*

Iris pallida 'Argentea Variegata'

Phlox paniculata 'Norah Leigh'

Polemonium caeruleum 'Brise d'Anjou'*

Polygonatum × *hybridum* 'Striatum'

Sinopodophyllum hexandrum

*suitable for pots

background or provide a backdrop for other plants. Fronds remain in place well into the autumn.

Grasses and others

Grasses come in a vast range of sizes and colours, including blue-green (*Festuca glauca*), red (*Imperata cylindrica* 'Rubra') and yellow-green (*Milium effusum* 'Aureum'). They look excellent grouped together or as specimens placed individually among flowering plants to add texture and form to a border. A great number of grasses provide interest in winter.

Many moisture-loving plants, including the large-leaved *Rodgersia podophylla*, the striking variegated iris *Iris pseudacorus* 'Variegata', Solomon's seal (*Polygonatum* × *hybridum*) and *Maianthemum racemosum,* have strongly architectural foliage that is useful for providing long-term structure in shady, damp places.

Vegetables, fruit and herbs

Nothing beats home-grown produce for taste and freshness, and once you've started growing your own you'll never look back. It gives a wonderful sense of achievement too. Even the smallest gardens can accommodate some edible plants – you can grow them among your ornamentals, or in raised beds or containers. Plant breeders have come up with 'mini' or 'baby' vegetables that are suitable for the tiniest of spaces.

Where to grow crops

If you've never grown vegetables, you might worry that they will look ugly and out of place in a small space, but a tiny, neat vegetable garden can be very attractive, as can vegetables in tubs or raised beds, where you can get higher yields. If you want a challenge, you could create a highly ornamental formal kitchen garden in a small space (*see* pages 76–7), while for just a few crops, simply slip plants in among the ornamentals in your borders, making sure they won't be too shaded or too close together. Your yield may not be huge, but it's still fun to graze on home-grown produce as you wander about the garden.

The ideal position for veg-growing is a sunny, sheltered site with rich, well-drained soil or compost.

Containers

Some vegetables and fruit are actually better off in containers, where you can provide them with exactly what they need. The key to

A hanging basket full of strawberries is attractive and protects the fruit from slug damage.

success is good-quality multipurpose compost and regular watering. With small plants, such as salad leaves and strawberries, try hanging baskets, which will keep away slugs and other pests. You can also grow peas like this, though the crop will be small.

Don't forget

For containers, choose the small, quick-maturing veg varieties specially recommended for pots. These are known as 'mini veg' and can be ready to eat in 6 to 12 weeks.

Strawberries, rhubarb, Swiss chard and carrots – looking very healthy and promising delicious crops – are growing in recycled but colour-matched containers.

Edible plants suitable for growing in containers

Apples	Cranberries
Apricots	Cucumbers
Aubergines	Figs
Beans (French beans, runner beans)	Grapes
	Herbs
Blueberries	Lettuces and salad leaves
Carrots	New potatoes
Cherries	Peaches
Citrus fruits (lemons, limes, oranges, grapefruit, calamondins)	Peppers (including chillies)
	Plums
Courgettes	Strawberries
	Tomatoes

Raised beds

Most traditional vegetables, as well as fruit and herbs, can be grown in raised beds. Make their sides about 30cm (12in) or more high and fill with a mixture of soil and well-rotted manure or garden compost. This provides a highly nutritious environment for your crops and means more crops for less space.

Growing vegetables

In a small area, you're unlikely to be able to supply yourself with all your vegetable needs, so concentrate on your favourites and those that are nicer when eaten really fresh, or more difficult to buy.

Raised beds encourage you to grow vegetables in neat blocks and rows, which produces great results in terms of appearance and yield.

Quick crops in small spaces

Crops that mature quickly and take up very little room are ideal for the novice gardener with a small garden. Salad leaves can be picked in as little as three weeks from sowing and do well in pots or small gaps. Plant climbing French beans and runners in late spring. They shoot up quickly, producing their prodigious crops over many weeks. Because they're tall and slender, they fit almost anywhere, as do mangetouts and sugarsnap peas, which crop in about two months.

Longer to wait

Tomatoes don't start to fruit until midsummer, but one well-tended plant in a sunny spot will supply you with a generous crop. Aubergines, peppers and chillies are best in pots, so ideal on a sunny patio. Spring onions are another easy crop and can be put into small gaps in flower beds. Carrots have pretty foliage that looks good anywhere. Grow early varieties and eat them as soon as they are the size of a finger.

If you want fresh winter veg, kale is a good choice. Some varieties, such as 'Black Tuscany', have lovely architectural leaves.

More space

Courgettes are excellent if you have the space. Just one plant will produce plenty to keep you supplied and they really are much better than in the shops. Globe artichokes are less generous with their crop but are attractive plants, perfect for putting in a flower bed.

What's easy to grow and what's not

EASY	EASY TO GET CROPS BUT NEED PRUNING		REQUIRE QUITE A LOT OF EFFORT AND EXPERIENCE
Courgettes		Cabbage	Sweetcorn
Garlic	Apples	Carrots	Tomatoes (cordon types)
Kale	Blackberries	Celeriac	Turnip
Leeks	Blackcurrants	Cherries	
New potatoes	Gooseberries	Citrus fruit (indoors over winter)	REQUIRE QUITE A LOT OF EFFORT AND EXPERIENCE
Onions and shallots	Loganberries	Cucumber	Apricots
Peppers and chillies	Raspberries	Figs	Calabrese
Perpetual spinach	Redcurrants	French beans	Cauliflowers
Rhubarb		Lettuce	Celery
Rocket	REQUIRE A LITTLE MORE EXPERIENCE	Pears	Florence fennel
Runner beans		Peas and mangetout	Grapes
Salad leaves	Artichokes	Plums	Kiwis
Spring onions	Aubergines	Pumpkins and squashes	Nectarines
Strawberries	Beetroot	Radishes	Peaches
Swiss chard	Broad beans	Swedes	Spinach
Tomatoes (bush)	Broccoli (sprouting)		

Cherries thrive against a warm wall, providing year-round decoration and, of course, summer fruits.

There is no excuse for not growing fruit. Stepover apples fit into the tiniest of spaces and crop well.

Growing fruit

Fruit is even easier to incorporate into an ornamental garden than vegetables, especially fruit trees, since many are very decorative and most are available on dwarfing rootstocks, which means they will never grow very large.

Fruit trees

Apples are among the most versatile and easy of all, producing good crops on plants from as small as 60cm (2ft) tall. Called stepovers, these diminutive plants are ideal for growing next to paths or along the borders of flower beds as a sort of low hedge or high edge. They need support in the form of posts and wires, but when properly tended will produce a reasonable number of normal-sized fruit.

Walls and fences can also accommodate apples, as well as pears, cherries, peaches, apricots, plums and even soft fruit such as blackcurrants or gooseberries. Here, the plants need to be trained with wires and canes as cordons, fans or espaliers. This does require some regular pruning and tying in, but the results can be spectacular when the plants are covered in blossom or fruit. Depending on the fruit grown, you will need to allow around 2.5m (8ft) of free space.

Small dill plants nestle among ornamental cabbages and flowering plants in this mixed border.

Cane fruit and vines

Canes, such as blackberries and loganberries, and vines, including grapes and kiwi fruit, can be grown on fences too, but are perhaps best when trained up and over pergolas and arches, where they will look pretty and their fruit will be within easy reach for harvesting. Choose thornless varieties of blackberries, such as 'Loch Ness', which is quite compact, or 'Veronique', which has pink flowers. Grapes are less easy to succeed with outdoors, but the more sheltered the garden, the better are your chances of a good crop. They need regular trimming to ensure they put their energy into fruit rather than foliage. The same goes for kiwis, which can be quite rampant but don't mind being cut back severely in late winter and again in summer. You need a male and female plant to get fruit.

Growing herbs

Most garden herbs double up as ornamentals and can be grown in flower beds and borders among the other plants. Chives, parsley, marjoram and thyme look pretty at the front of borders, where they work well as a low-growing 'hedge', while rosemary, dill and fennel are good structural plants. Coriander and basil will do best if they are grown in containers in a sheltered situation, and mints should also be kept in pots, sunk into the ground, to prevent unwanted spread.

With their large leaves and strong shapes, exotic plants are *de rigeur* for jungle gardens. However, in small quantities, they also have a place in minimalist modern-style gardens and even cottage gardens, since cottage gardeners traditionally try growing almost anything they can lay their hands on. Many plants that are not in reality exotic can have an exotic character, so the choice is wide.

Big leaves

One of the most remarkable things about many exotic plants is the size of their leaves, which are often head-turners. The huge paddles of the bananas (*Musa*) are superb, as are the enormous arching fronds produced by the tree ferns (*Dicksonia* is the most hardy). Cannas are rather like smaller, more upright bananas; their leaves may be red-purple ('King Humbert') or striped ('Striata') and they also have vivid flowers in a variety of colours late in the year.

Fatsia japonica and *Ricinus communis* have leaves with deeply cut lobes, like many-fingered hands. The fatsia is good for a shady spot, where it will thrive if sheltered as well. *Ricinus* or castor-oil plant is available in red-

Usually it is the size, shape and form of foliage that makes us think of plants as being exotic.

① The mainstay of the exotic garden, bananas are strongly architectural yet never overpowering.
② *Fatsia japonica* has huge, glossy leaves that make a great impact.
③ The slim, grassy foliage of *Arundo donax* whispers in the breeze.

leaved versions, such as 'Carmencita', which also has red flowers. These are both large plants (4m/13ft), but *Tetrapanax papyrifer* is even bigger, at up to 5m (16ft), with leaves about 50cm (20in) across. However, cold winters tend to keep it in check.

Tropical shapes

To most of us on these cool islands, palm trees are icons of the tropics, yet some palms are, amazingly, hardy enough to grow outside here. The Chusan palm (*Trachycarpus fortunei*) has large, fan-shaped leaves, while the fronds of the jelly palm (*Butia capitata*) are longer and reminiscent of those of the coconut.

The tender biennial *Echium pininana* shoots up as high as 4m (13ft), but it is comparatively narrow. Its leafy stems produce thousands of blue flowers, after which it dies. *Geranium maderense* is smaller but still impressive, making clumps of glossy, divided leaves and large, loose heads of purple-pink flowers. For a hint of tropical sugarcane plantation, grow the giant reed (*Arundo donax*), which has grassy stems up to 5m (16ft) high. It has variegated and striped versions for a lighter effect.

More exotic plants

Agapanthus (African lily)*	*Hedychium* (gingers)*
Amaranthus caudatus	*Hosta**
	Kniphofia
*Begonia**	*Lobelia cardinalis* 'Queen Victoria'
Bergenia (elephant's ears)	*Phormium**
*Brugmansia**	*Rhus typhina*
Chamaerops humilis	*Rodgersia*
*Cordyline**	*Salvia**
Dahlia	*Solenostemon* (coleus)*
Eriobotrya	*Zinnia**
Farfugium	
Gunnera	**suitable for pots**

Don't forget

Many exotic plants are not fully hardy and will need protection over winter, but some are proving much tougher than originally thought.

Specific situations

If you have an outdoor space – however tiny – and a bit of
determination, then you have the basics you need to create
a garden. All over the world, people manage to produce floral
displays or grow crops in the most unpromising situations and
under the most difficult conditions, from dark alleyways and
dingy basements to narrow steps, sunburnt courtyards and
windswept balconies. If you want a garden, you need stop at
nothing to achieve it!

Windowsills

Even the tiniest of outdoor spaces, such as a windowsill, provides an opportunity to garden. With window boxes you'll need to choose your plants carefully and be prepared to change them regularly, but you can have something to nurture, look at and enjoy through all the seasons. With a bit of ingenuity you'll find plenty of ways to make wonderful, colourful displays.

White-flowered cyclamen, winter cherry and variegated ivy create a picture in this winter window box.

Seasonal displays

In spring and summer you'll be spoilt for choice with plants for containers. The autumn and winter months are more challenging, but it is still possible to have something pretty to look at.

For spring displays, make the most of tiny flowering bulbs, such as *Iris* 'Joyce'. Along with hyacinths, these are often sold in individual pots and are easy to fit into containers among permanent plants. In summer, choose fragrant nemesias, such as 'Vanilla Scent', as well as the huge-flowered begonias, which include the popular 'Apricot Shades'. These will flower well into autumn if the weather is settled.

Windowsill plants in autumn include cyclamens (*Cyclamen hederifolium*) and small bedding chrysanthemums. Plant them among small, variegated ivies, such as *Hedera* 'Glacier', for a longer-lasting display, since the ivies should survive winter. Refresh winter baskets and window boxes with small skimmias, such as the berrying *Skimmia japonica* 'Rogersii', heathers and tiny conifers. But beware, these conifers will eventually grow too large for pots. Don't overlook the potential of dried flowers, seeds and fruit, and twiggy branches, which

can be sprayed different colours. You can add seasonal fairy lights and other outdoor decorations.

Practicalities

To have a successful window box you need adequate access so that you can tend the plants easily and safely, it's also important that the plants don't stop you opening the windows. Any pots and containers must be carefully secured so that they cannot fall off or topple over, particularly from high windowsills.

Strong garden wire and sturdy brackets will come in handy, as will fixings designed for brick or concrete. If your sills are narrow, it might be better to attach the containers to the walls below or beside them or use hanging baskets instead, which are usually less likely to cause an obstruction.

For information on how to plant a basic container, *see* page 54.

If you provide the right conditions, you can even recreate a flowering meadow on your windowsill.

This spacious box contains mixed herbs and flowers, including tiny strawberries and nasturtiums.

Front gardens

Front gardens are frequently undervalued and neglected. They are often the repository for all sorts of rubbish and are most usually seen as a convenient place to park the car. However, it is becoming increasingly obvious that they are valuable assets, especially where they are the only outdoor space available.

Using plants

There's no reason your front garden can't be every bit as attractive as your back garden. Try to include as many plants as you can, especially close to the road if possible, where they can act as a barrier to wind and noise and dirt. If pollution is a problem, choose pollution-tolerant varieties, such as *Berberis thunbergii*, *Escallonia* and *Buddleja davidii* cultivars. Planting vegetation instead of covering the soil with tarmac or

This modern house has a formal, stylish front garden of grasses and succulents. It looks attractive and provides a screen from passers-by.

concrete also reduces the risk of flooding (*see* opposite); wildlife will appreciate it too.

As with other gardens, it's important to create a basic structure around which shorter-lived displays can perform. You may not be able to fit in a tree, but you could perhaps put in a shrub or two. Evergreens such as box, strawberry tree (*Arbutus*), pieris and yew (*Taxus*) are ideal and can be clipped to keep them within bounds.

Make the walls work hard, too. Put up a trellis or other support, preferably one that doubles as an

A conifer hedge blocks out noise and, along with magnolias in box cubes, screens the road. In this restful garden, neat forms create a gentle rhythm.

attractive element in its own right, and plant a climber or two (*see* pages 92–6). Evergreen climbers are useful for year-round interest and you can grow annual climbers through them for seasonal colour. Even if you have only a doorstep you could still include a few pots by the entrance.

Greener parking

In the past few decades, as car ownership has risen, it has become increasingly common to tarmac over the front garden to create a drive. While this is understandable, it has led to problems of flooding, as in periods of heavy rainfall the water just sits on the surface rather than being absorbed by vegetation. If you need to have a drive, use gravel or another porous material to reduce the chance of flooding. There are also several other options available.

Permeable paving From blocks to bricks, the characteristic that unites permeable paving is that it allows water to drain through, usually because the joints are not mortared and the paving sits on a bed of sand.

Combination surfaces Concrete slabs, setts or cobbles are laid in conjunction with loose materials, particularly gravel, to create an attractive, free-draining and practical surface.

Reinforced grass Although plastic honeycomb-type mats are useful, for permanent parking waffle or egg-box design concrete slabs are better. The concrete takes the weight of the car and the holes are filled with gravel or soil and planted with grass.

For an alternative driveway, set strips of concrete into grass. The weight of the car is borne by the concrete and the grass absorbs rainwater.

A front garden can be as decorative as a back garden. Here, foxgloves, roses, poppies, lupins and *Sisyrinchium striatum*, among others, create a beautiful display.

Balconies and roof gardens

Roof gardens and balconies are a mixed blessing for plants and people. They are valuable outdoor spaces, but generally exposed to at least one and often all of the climatic extremes: buffeting wind, baking sun, freezing cold and lashing rain. For gardeners there are also the challenges of importing heavy potting compost and enough water to keep the plants alive.

Balcony gardens

The most important first step in creating a balcony garden is to lower the wind speed, which will in turn help to prevent some of the more extreme conditions. A well-placed screen (*see* pages 33–4) should do the trick. One that can be moved on runners depending on the wind direction is even more useful. Although trellis or brushwood screens would do the job, it's worth splashing out on glass, since this will keep out the wind but not the sun. If your balcony is very sunny, coloured or frosted glass will reduce the glare without making the space too dark.

The other major factor to bear in mind on a balcony is weight. It's important not to overburden the balcony with heavy pots, which will only get heavier when full of plants and well watered. Choose light containers made from Glass Reinforced Plastic (*see* pages 52–3) rather than ceramic or concrete, and loamless potting compost, which is lighter than loam-based. Put polystyrene chips or packaging in the bottom in place of traditional drainage crocks; this will reduce the amount of compost you need and keep the weight down. Add water-retaining crystals to avoid

A metal framework supports a wisteria screen and colourful pelargoniums on this imaginative balcony garden.

drought and slow-release food to ensure your plants never go hungry.

The major disadvantage of plastic containers is that they may be top-heavy when planted. Make sure you secure them carefully so there's no chance of taller plants falling over the edge of the balcony or against your windows or door.

Successful planting

Even on a balcony, the rule of having a few structural plants and some fillers holds true (*see* pages 78–109). Select one or two plants for impact, then dress them up through the seasons using colourful annuals and other small ornamental plants.

Drought-resistant plants and a piece of driftwood used as a decorative sculpture set the scene on this balcony with its wonderful view.

Roof gardens

When it comes to wind, roof gardens are often worse hit than balconies. The wind may come from all directions and will be much stronger than at ground level. However, some carefully placed (and securely fixed) screens will reduce its impact. If the roof is very open, perforated screens that act as windbreaks and can support one or two plants are better than solid ones, which can cause the wind to eddy around your plants.

Your roof garden is likely to get plenty of light. Although plants and people like sunlight, a little shade is equally important. The interplay between light and shade helps to create visual interest (*see* page 12) and structures that produce shade will also create an appealing feeling of seclusion, as well as providing privacy (*see* pages 22–3). Try to include a pergola, arbour or even just an awning, making sure they're attached very securely, of course. For an intimate effect, it's important that structures like these are higher than your head, but they don't necessarily need to be something you can sit under.

Planting

As with balconies, the key to a safe and successful roof garden is to keep everything as light as possible and to make sure there is no chance of plants or pots falling off the roof. This is a tough environment, since the temperature will plummet at night and it will often be hot and dry during the day. However, with a bit of care it is possible to find a good selection of plants that will cope with these conditions.

Trellis screening and a pergola have made this roof garden a secluded, tranquil spot in the heart of the city. The plants include euphorbia, clematis, strawberries and roses.

Plants for windy sites

Astelia chathamica
Calamagrostis 'Karl Foerster'
Cordyline australis
Dianthus
Lavandula
Libertia grandiflora
Pennisetum alopecuroides 'Hameln'
Phormium tenax
Pinus mugo 'Mops'
Prunus laurocerasus
Rosmarinus officinalis
Sedum (low-growing types)
Sempervivum
Stipa tenuissima
Taxus baccata
Thymus
Trachycarpus fortunei

Basements and side passages

Basement courtyards or light wells and alleys down the sides of buildings tend to be shady, but unless it's pitch dark, there are quite a few plants that will survive in the dank and gloom. The main challenge with these sites is making them appealing for people, so think about how you might use the space before you start to plan the plants. If your basement is sunny, *see* Courtyards, pages 118–19, for inspiration.

Pale blue trellis screens and neatly trimmed box plants transform a basement into an elegant courtyard.

Brightening basements

Start by making the area as bright as possible with light-coloured hard landscaping materials and pale-coloured paints. Opt for cream, pale honey yellow, soft brown or mushroom pink, since these will both warm and lighten the space. White can be somewhat harsh and cool, but if you want a sophisticated effect, it's a good choice, along with pale grey. Go for matt finishes for high walls and fences to avoid a public-convenience look, but choose shiny ones for paving and any low-level walls. These will reflect light, which will make the area seem brighter; they will also produce semi-reflections of other objects in the vicinity, so subtly increasing the sense of space. (*See also* Towering walls, page 119.)

Adding ornament

Look for decorative and practical items that will increase the light and blur the boundaries (*see* page 16). Mirrors are excellent. You don't have to be able to see into them: put them up high or down low, or use them at angles and in tandem to work like a periscope. Coloured glass can also be very effective (position it to produce interesting colour plays), and choose shiny watering cans, pots, plant supports and furniture wherever you get the chance.

Lighting

Electric lighting can transform otherwise unusable dark corners (*see* pages 20 and 56–7). You wouldn't baulk at lighting a dark

Shade-tolerant plants for dark, narrow spaces

Akebia quinata
Berberidopsis corallina
Clematis 'Nelly Moser'
Cotoneaster horizontalis
Hedera colchica cultivars
Hedera helix cultivars
Humulus lupulus 'Aureus'
Impatiens (busy Lizzie)
Parthenocissus henryana
Taxus baccata 'Fastigiata'
Vinca

Quarry-tiled steps flanked with lush green plants, including *Fatsia japonica*, welcome you to this basement flat.

room during the day, so don't feel guilty about doing the same in the garden. You can make the lights obvious and decorative, which will work well if you tend to use the garden in the evening, or be more discreet, perhaps disguising them so that it looks as if chinks of sunlight are coming in from elsewhere. Use outdoor-safe fixings with long-life, low-energy bulbs and always hire a professional to install outdoor lighting from mains electricity.

Planting in basements

Your planting options will be increased if you can use large containers or even build raised beds (*see* page 42) in your basement. Fill these with a mixture of peat-free and loam-based potting composts. This will allow a wider range of plants, particularly larger ones, to thrive. Make maximum use of walls and fences for hanging baskets and small containers as well as climbers.

If the area is very dark, you may have to settle for foliage plants (*see* page 105), although there are one or two flowering ones that may just perform (*see* box, opposite). On mild days in summer, you could move some of your house plants outside to brighten the display, since many of these are suited to low light levels.

Enlivening side passages

Because of their narrowness, side passages are most likely to be seen through a window or in passing, rather than sat in, so concentrate on making the space comfortable for plants and attractive to look at from where you will most often see it. If the passage is gloomy, begin by

White walls have lightened this narrow area, making a wonderful backdrop for climbers and wall shrubs and highlighting the pale colours of annuals in pots.

making it as light as possible, in the same way as you would a basement.

Passages are often draughty and screens (*see* pages 33–4) are the best way to reduce the 'wind-tunnel' effect (*see* page 60). Be particular about where you place them: analyse which direction the wind most frequently comes from and where it picks up speed. Often this will be at the passage entrance, but you might be able to divert it beforehand, so you won't need to put a screen where it will further decrease light levels and might reduce access.

Planting in side passages

Assuming the space is longish and narrowish and bordered on both sides by fencing or walls, it is sensible to stick with small plants and climbers (*see* opposite and

pages 92–6). If you're lucky enough to have a narrow soil border, make the most of it by digging in a bag or two of farmyard manure (sterilized types are sold in garden centres and do not smell). Otherwise, consider making a narrow raised bed and filling this with a peat-free and loam-based compost. Fix trellis or wires to the wall or fence that receives the most light and train climbers onto these (*see* page 33). Add to the display at different times of the year by hanging pots of flowering plants, nestled among the climbers.

Don't forget

Add interest and a touch of whimsy by using *trompe l'oeil* trellis panels (see page 21), perhaps containing a mirror or a small painted scene, or wall-mounted ornaments swathed in climbers.

Courtyards

A courtyard should be a wonderful place to grow plants and sit out in. However, such spaces are often surrounded by high walls or overlooked from above, making you feel a bit like a caged animal when you're outside. Because they're enclosed, they're often very sheltered, which is great for growing cold-sensitive plants, but if they're sunny this can make them sweltering in hot weather. Luckily, there are ways to overcome these problems.

Hard landscaping

Even in a tiny, building-bound courtyard, many of the basic principles of garden design come in handy (*see* pages 10–21). Begin by carefully assessing the space and take into account its various practical roles. Good quality, well-planned hard landscaping will go a long way

Decorative pots and a classical statue play important roles in this mainly foliage-based garden, which includes hydrangea, wisteria and mimosa.

A simple trellis frames the cool planting and provides an extra dimension in this tiny space.

towards making the area attractive and this, in turn, will make it more likely that you will enjoy using it. Replace ugly concrete with gravel, paving, bricks or decking (*see* pages 37–40). Repoint and paint old brick walls and renew flaking render or disguise it with trellis or other wall-mounted frames that can be used for climbing plants or simply for providing decoration in their own right (*see* pages 32–4).

Dividing and sheltering

In a really tiny area, disguising boundaries (*see* page 16) becomes even more important. Use trellis, mirrors and false archways to give the impression of more space, just out of sight. Even the shadows created by a plain piece of trellis fixed directly to a wall will add an extra dimension. Although there may not be room for the traditional structures used for dividing a garden, such as pergolas or arches, you could hint at these with a row of cantilevered beams and one or two upright posts, fixed to the wall or floor.

Even if the sun doesn't beat down all day on your courtyard, provide yourself with a little shade or shelter: light and shade increase the feeling of space and seclusion in any garden (see page 12). In a minute area, consider an awning or umbrella, both of which can be folded away when not in use. In a sunny courtyard, these work well in dark colours to provide deep shade from the hot sun; in a darker space, use bright colours, such as yellow and orange, which will increase the feeling of light and provide privacy without producing too much shade. If your courtyard is shady, the advice on basements on pages 116–17 can offer more inspiration.

Towering walls

The walls surrounding courtyards often tower well above head height and can be two or three storeys high. Although this may increase the sense of seclusion, it can also be rather claustrophobic. One of the best ways to reduce this effect is to decorate the walls up to 2m (6ft) or so. This will concentrate your focus on the lower part of the wall, helping you to forget the full height. Try to avoid too much fussy detail, because this will reduce any feeling of space, and go for large, simple blocks of colour instead. In the right setting, a trompe l'oeil scene (see page 21) would also work very well.

Planting in courtyards

If there is no open ground, create raised beds (see page 42) and use largish containers (see pages 52–5),

designing the planting as if they were borders to create a cohesive and pleasing display. For information on planting containers, see page 54.

Sunny courtyard

The choice of plants, as always, depends on your taste and the ambience you want to create. You could fill a sunny space with lush tropical plants to produce a jungle effect (see pages 74–5 and 109), or be more restrained and recreate the simple courtyards found in many European cities, with just one or two climbers, particularly jasmine, and a spot of colour provided by the ubiquitous pelargonium. Alternatively, you might like a Mexican-style courtyard, with large agave cacti and a backdrop of brightly coloured walls (see right).

Shady courtyard

Shade- and moisture-loving plants, such as hydrangeas, Solomon's seal (Polygonatum) and ferns, should do nicely in a shady courtyard, and

Bright colours and spiky plants – here Beschorneria yuccoides – evoke the ambience of a hot, dry desert.

busy lizzies (Impatiens) are surprisingly well able to cope with shade (see also page 116). Inevitably, deep shade is a difficult prospect for many plants, so be prepared to replace them if they become lanky and sick through lack of light.

This stylish courtyard garden has everything – interesting hard landscaping, lovely plants, a secluded seating area and a tiny pool.

Gardens of newly built houses are usually one of two things: empty or superficially landscaped. Although you might not believe it now, the former is better than the latter, as it allows you to create a garden that is entirely your own. A garden landscaped by the builders may be welcome at first, but it is unlikely to be to your taste and there could be all sorts of hidden problems, such as dreadful drainage and buried rubbish, awaiting discovery.

Take a look at your soil: in new-build gardens it is often imported, of poor quality and not usually very deep.

Enclose the space

As with any garden, deciding where to start is always the first hurdle, but it is usually easiest to begin by defining the boundaries (*see* pages 32–5), if this has not already been done for you. As soon as you have a fence, wall or the beginnings of a hedge in place, the garden will start to feel more like your own. Even if you haven't decided exactly what sort of boundaries you want, it's important to claim the space with temporary markers, such as cheap and cheerful fence panels. This will also allow you to see it more clearly: its basic shape, as well as any views you

might like to enhance or eyesores you may want to disguise and so on; you will immediately start to get ideas for the rest of the garden.

Preparing the site

As soon as you can, assess your site and draw up a plan for the garden (*see* pages 59–67). If possible, install the hard landscaping before you plant the flower beds. Next, set out the flower beds and borders. Before you plant anything, you'll need to take a really good look at the soil.

The biggest problem with soil on a recent building site is that drainage is

likely to be poor. This is because of compaction caused by traffic – human and vehicular – moving over the area during construction. Buried rubble, such as chunks of concrete and broken bricks, is also common. Although the builders may do a clear-up at the end of the job, there will probably still be plenty left under the surface.

Improving drainage in the garden

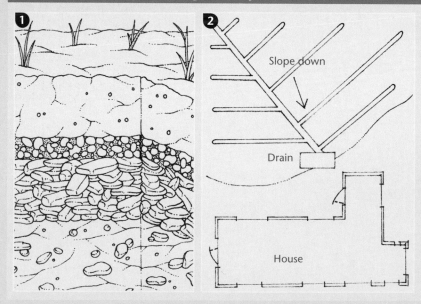

1

2

Slope down

Drain

House

If you have really bad drainage in the garden it may well be worth installing a drainage system. There are two main types – a simple soakaway system and a herringbone drainage system.

① A simple soakaway system improves drainage on a flat site. Excavate the poorly drained area to a depth of 35cm (14in) and spread a layer of rubble 15cm (6in) deep. On top of this add a layer of gravel or coarse sand 5cm (2in) deep, then replace the topsoil so that it is at least 15cm (6in) deep all over.

On a sloping site, soakaway pits with a greater depth of rubble and sand can be used. They can be sited in the lowest part of the garden, allowing water to trickle away without sitting on the surface of the soil or lawn.

② A herringbone drainage system needs to be installed by a professional water engineer. Drainage pipes and rubble are laid underground. They're connected to an existing drainage system and excess water is taken away from the site.

To alleviate compaction, dig over areas where you plan to have flower beds or a lawn to at least 45cm (18in). Add lots of well-rotted manure or other humus-rich material to improve drainage and increase the soil's nutritional value. Where drainage is still poor, you could install a soakaway or herringbone drainage system (*see* opposite). This isn't cheap but will be a permanent solution. Alternatively, in areas that are poorly drained grow moisture-loving plants or install raised beds (*see* page 42).

If the soil is simply poor quality – stony, clumpy, very sandy – you can buy topsoil in bags or by the lorry-load. Use a recommended supplier, as the quality can be variable.

Adding the plants

Start by planting a range of structural plants, since these will create the backbone of your garden. Next, add climbers and wall shrubs and then the filler plants (*see* pages 84–105). Many annuals do well on poor soil, so for quick-fix colour in flower beds and borders – especially if you arrive in spring and want flowers for summer – consider scattering seed in blocks and seeing what comes up (*see* right).

(*see* pages 84–105)

Builders' landscaping

Beware of ready-landscaped gardens. The plants may look good until the weather is very dry or very wet, when leaves may wilt or turn yellow and plants may die, indicating poor planting, poor-quality plants or poor drainage. If you want to keep them, dig around existing plants as deeply as possible to loosen the surrounding compacted soil and allow the roots to spread. Add plenty of organic matter, for instance well-rotted manure, to the soil to improve drainage as well as feed the plants and help them to establish.

Annuals are excellent for filling an empty space with colour and they do it relatively quickly.

① Bright orange California poppies (*Eschscholzia californica*) look good with pale love-in-a-mist (*Nigella damascena* 'Miss Jekyll').

② Cornflowers (*Centaurea cyanus*) flower from midsummer into autumn.

③ Field poppies (*Papaver rhoeas*) are excellent for early-summer colour.

④ Corncockle (*Agrostemma githago*) has prettily marked pink-purple flowers.

Fast-growing annuals

Agrostemma githago (corncockle)

Calendula officinalis (pot marigold)

Centaurea cyanus (cornflower)

Chrysanthemum carinatum

Eschscholzia californica (California poppy)

Gypsophila elegans (baby's breath)

Linaria maroccana (toadflax)

Lobularia maritima (sweet alyssum)

Matthiola bicornis (night-scented stock)

Nicotiana (tobacco plant)

Nigella damascena (love-in-a-mist)

Papaver rhoeas (field poppy)

Papaver somniferum (opium poppy)

Schizanthus pinnatus (poor man's orchid)

Tagetes (marigold)

Tropaeolum speciosum (flame creeper)

Index

Acknowledgements

BBC Books and OutHouse would like to thank the following for their assistance in preparing this book: Phil McCann for advice and guidance; Robin Whitecross for picture research; Lindsey Brown for proofreading; June Wilkins for the index.

Picture credits

Key t = top, b = bottom, l = left, r = right, c = centre

PHOTOGRAPHS

All photographs by Jonathan Buckley except those listed below.

GAP Photos Anne Green-Armytage 42; Adrian Bloom 84t; Mark Bolton 94tr; Elke Borkowski 12t, 16, 27t, 49l, 79, 81, 91(2), 99, 87l; Marion Brenner 15; Nicola Browne 20t, 22b, 52t, 53b; Keith Burdett 93c; Leigh Clapp 17b, 80t; Sarah Cuttle 85l, 119b; Julie Dansereau 90c; Frederic Didillon 34tl; Heather Edwards 86c; Ron Evans 86l; FhF Greenmedia 96bc; GAP Photos 45(1); Suzie Gibbons 33b, 40; John Glover 18, 21(2) & (3), 23, 80b, 96tr, 103b, 104b, 111br, 113b, 114b, 116t; Jerry Harpur 20b, 26b, 27b, 30, 35(3), 47, 53tl, 53tr, 56(1), 57(1), 57(3), 62, 111t, 113t, 113b, 116b; Marcus Harpur 25b, 48(1), 48(2), 84b, 102tl; Charles Hawes 55tl; Neil Holmes 88r; Michael Howes 88c; Martin Hughes-Jones 85r, 93b; Janet Johnson 25t; Lynn Keddie 102b; Geoff Kidd 89r, 109(2); Michael King 49r; Fiona Lea 37r, 109(3), 121(4); Jenny Lilly 87c; Fiona McLeod 26t; Zara Napier 87r; Clive Nichols 13b, 21(1), 35t, 44, 46br, 57(2), 57(4), 86r, 106b, 111bl, 118t; Hanneke Reijbroek 114t; Howard Rice 55tr; Martin Schroder 37ct; JS Sira 17t, 37cb, 83b, 91bl, 94tc, 96br; Graham Strong 88l; Maddie Thornhill 101b; Juliette Wade 39b; Rob Whitworth 19, 34b, 45(3), 89l; Steven Wooster 22t

Andrew McIndoe 58, 95tr

David Austin Roses 93l

Marianne Majerus Garden Images Steve Gunther 112t, 112b, 115, 117, 118b, 119t; Andrew Lawson 93r, 95tc, 96b, 97(4), 110; Marianne Majerus 2–3, 4, 5, 21(3), 31, 32, 46t, 48t, 52bl, 52bc, 55br, 91(1)

The Garden Collection Andrew Lawson 108b

Sue Gordon 35(1)

Raymond Turner 45(2)

Robin Whitecross 58

ILLUSTRATIONS

Julia Cady 47

Caroline De Lane Lea 28–9, 65, 69, 71, 73, 75, 77

Lizzie Harper 38, 39, 42, 43, 44, 51, 60, 120

Janet Tanner 49

Thanks are also due to the following designers and owners, whose gardens appear in the book:

Clare Agnew 34b; Lee Belgrau 17t; Berzi and Casares 30; Jean Bird 21(1); Nigel Boardman and Stephen Gelly 25t; Kathy Brown, The Manor House, Stevington, Bedfordshire 52bl; Declan Buckley 22b, 119t; David Chase, West Green Cottage, Hampshire 46bl; Laurie Chetwood and Patrick Collins 45(3); Ruth Collier 21(3); Henrietta Courtauld 112b; Stuart Craine 5r; 48t; Stephen Crisp 114b, 116t; Veronica Cross, Lower Hopton Farm, Herefordshire 100b; Katherine Crouch, Somerset 8; Tigger Cullinan 2–3; Duotuin Rotterdam, Holland 114t; Stephen Firth, RHS Chelsea Flower Show 2005 35bc; Simon Fraser 62; Adam Frost 42; Diarmuid Gavin 56b; John Glover 111br; Judith Glover 40; Anthony Goff, Spencer Road, London 13; Graham Gough, Marchants Hardy Plants, East Sussex 24t; Grafton Cottage, Staffordshire 96b; Isobelle C Greene 26b; Justin Greer 48(1), 84b; Mark Gregory 46br; Roger Griffen 35(3); Luciano Guibillei 57(1); Bunny Guinness 61; Nada Habet 55tl; Hannath garden, London 80t; Harpak Design 119b; Henrietta Courtauld 112b; Bernard Hicks 20t; Jamie Higham 48(2); Iona Hilleary Landscape Design 26t; Catherine Horwood 115; Elaine Hughes 25b; Susie Ind 111t; Paul Kelly, Church Lane, London 9, 34tc; John Keyes 116b; Christopher Lloyd, Great Dixter, East Sussex 83 tc & r, 100tl, 109; Francoise Maas 5l; Angela Mainwaring, Hampton Court Palace Flower Show 2002 21(2); Steve Martino 53tr; Clare Matthews 57(4), 111bl; Graham McCleary/Natural Habitat 27b; Claire Mee 35tr; Peter Nixon 20b; Anthony Noel 118b; Roger Oates, Long Barn, Herefordshire 12b; The Old Vicarage, East Ruston, Norfolk 55br; Orange Street Studios 112t; Ross Palmer 52t, 53b; Dan Pearson, London 10; Sarah Raven, Perch Hill, East Sussex 11b, 54b, 82l, 102tr, 108tl, 121t; RHS Garden Hyde Hall 52bc; Jilayne Rickards 46t; Sara Jane Rothwell 31, 32; Charlotte Rowe 57(2); Amir Schlezinger of MyLandscapes for Lea Harrison 57(3); Vladimir Sitta 113t; Carol and Malcolm Skinner, Eastgrove Cottage Garden Nursery, Worcestershire 105br; Juliet Stafford 49r; Sue and Wol Staines, Glen Chantry, Essex 100tr, 107; Rita Streitz 91(1); Tom Stuart-Smith 82r, 101tl & r; Joe Swift and Sam Joyce 11t, 41; Christoph Swinnen 53tl; Thomasina Tarling 110, 117; Jo Thompson 19; Turn End 17b; Nick Walker, RHS Show Tatton Park 37cb; Donald Walsh 56(1); Claire Warnock and Rachel Watts 106b; Gay Wilson, Merton Hall Road, London 50b, 59b; Christian Wright 44; Diana Yakeley 4; Helen Yemm, Eldenhurst, East Sussex 78

While every effort has been made to trace and acknowledge all copyright holders, the publisher would like to apologize should there be any errors or omissions.